COMMUNICATION SKILLS HANDBOOK

THIRD EDITION

JANE **SUMMERS**
BRETT **SMITH**

WILEY

John Wiley & Sons Australia, Ltd

Third edition published 2010 by
John Wiley & Sons Australia, Ltd
42 McDougall Street, Milton Qld 4064

First published 1995 by the Faculty of Business & Commerce,
The University of Southern Queensland
Second edition 1997
Third edition 2001
Fourth edition 2001

First published by John Wiley & Sons Australia, Ltd 2002
Revised and updated edition published 2004

© J.Summers and B.Smith 1995, 1997, 2001, 2002, 2004, 2006, 2010

The moral rights of the authors have been asserted.

National Library of Australia
Cataloguing-in-Publication entry

Author:	Summers, Jane
Title:	Communications skills handbook/ Jane Summers, Brett Smith.
Edition:	3rd ed.
ISBN:	9780470820513 (pbk.)
Notes:	Includes index. Bibliography
Subjects:	Communication in accounting. Written communication. Oral communication.
Other Authors/Contributors:	Smith, Brett
Dewey Number:	657.014

Cover and internal design images: Wiley Art Studio

Cartoons by Shane Collinge

Typeset in India by diacriTech

Printed in China by
Printplus Limited

10 9 8 7 6

Contents

LIST OF TABLES

LIST OF FIGURES

Preface

This handbook is designed to assist university students at all levels to prepare and present written and verbal material. It does not claim to be comprehensive but rather attempts to deal with the major problems students are likely to encounter in the preparation and presentation of work for assessment. The handbook also aims to minimise potential problems of inconsistency in requirements among different departments, faculties and universities. By outlining a series of standard expectations and formats for written and verbal material in Australian universities, we hope to alleviate some of the confusion expressed by many students. For ease of use as a ready reference, this new edition is spiral bound and features chapter tabs, further enhancing the handbook style of the text.

Although this book attempts to provide an overview of generally accepted standards in terms of communication and presentation of assessable work, inevitably there will be minor variations between the guidelines presented here and the specific requirements for particular courses of study. Students are therefore strongly advised to consult their individual instructors for any specific guidelines they may require. Where no advice on formatting or style is available, we suggest that students use the information presented in the following pages.

For more detailed guidance on preparing and presenting written reports and assignments, the Commonwealth Government's *Style manual* (2002, now in its sixth edition) has long been regarded as the standard work of reference for all authors, editors and printers in Australia. To assist students, a quick reference guide to the *Style manual* is included in Chapter 1.

In addition to the chapters that deal with preparation and presentation of material for assessment, this book also includes techniques and tips to assist students to prepare for, and sit examinations and a chapter that will guide graduates and others in their quest for employment.

This handbook has received overwhelming endorsement from both students and staff since its inception in 1995. Amendments and improvements are constantly being made to ensure that it remains current while maintaining its brevity and relevance. To this end, we are always grateful for feedback from university students or staff.

Jane Summers
Brett Smith
March 2009

Objectives

The objectives of this handbook are:

- to provide students with guidelines that are consistent across their university studies and to outline the minimum requirements for formal presentation of written and verbal assignments

- to assist university staff to apply a consistent approach to the assessment of formally presented written and verbal material by students, irrespective of university, department, course or level of study

- to reinforce among students the view that communication skills are an integral component of their studies and essential to their careers, rather than optional skills isolated from their chosen disciplines.

Explanation of symbols

The following symbols are used throughout this book to highlight features that have proved particularly useful for students:

 Hints

 Examples of concepts being discussed

About the authors

Dr Jane Summers is the Associate Dean Learning and Teaching in the Faculty of Business at the University of Southern Queensland. She has spent many years both as a marketing practitioner and as an academic. Her teaching and research interests are in the areas of consumer behaviour, e-marketing and sports marketing.

Brett Smith has been a practitioner in business systems and technology for more than two and a half decades, during which time he has relied heavily on well-developed communication skills to formulate and communicate business systems solutions. His career has spanned both the corporate and academic sectors and he holds three degrees in business and technology related areas. Brett currently provides business systems consulting services to the corporate sector through his company, BisVision Australia.

Acknowledgements

This handbook uses recommendations and examples from a range of sources. In particular, we acknowledge the input and advice from the staff of the Faculties of Business, Commerce and Arts at the University of Southern Queensland and, for guides to layout and content, the Business Studies Department of the University of Queensland, Gatton College. Original conceptual ideas for this style of book for use by university students came from the work of Dr Jane Summers and Mr Cec Pederson while at Gatton College in 1993. Additional material and examples have been drawn from the sources listed in the List of References. The authors would also like to thank Rae Wear and Tricia Rooney for their valuable contributions to the creation and publication of the first edition of this book.

The following individuals also deserve mention for their specific contributions to earlier editions of this handbook: Cec Pedersen, for his input into the sections on case studies and report writing; Dr Lesley Willcoxon for her help with the referencing section; Professor Chad Perry for his contribution to the section on thesis writing and for other general style comments; the late Frank Jarvis for his input into the examination techniques section; and Dr Meredith Lawley for her contributions to the general guidelines section.

1 | Guidelines for assessment

1.1 Introduction

When preparing and presenting written material, a number of key areas will, if tackled conscientiously, help both to make the process easier and to increase the chances of achieving a satisfactory mark. The following points are universally accepted as applying to all written work, including assignments, reports, case studies, essays, books and journal articles.

Writing for assessment or review is a means of communicating ideas or demonstrating analytical skills or both in a structured way. Generally, the purpose of a written assignment is to inform the readers, to persuade them to consider a point of view and possibly to solve a problem or provide recommendations for future action. It is not an opportunity for free-form self-expression.

1.2 Assignment preparation guidelines

Writing for assessment can be daunting, and students may be tempted to procrastinate, believing they can complete a satisfactory product the night before the due date. Such last-minute efforts are obvious to any marker. The following hints may prove helpful in making writing less arduous.

If you have a choice of topic for your assignments, be sure to choose one that appeals to your imagination and interest. This will make any research or study much easier.

Try to find out exactly what the instructor is looking for:

1. Read and reread the assignment information carefully and thoughtfully.

2. Read all guidance and instructions you are given relating to the assignment, particularly information relating to layout and format.

3. Find the relevant sections in your assigned text and read these for increased understanding.

4. Listen to any audiotape instructions provided.

5. Research the topic using library and Internet resources (being careful to record the source of information for later referencing — see chapter 2).

6. Share your views with other students in study groups, tutorial groups or electronic discussion groups where these are available, but remember that unless the assignment has been nominated as a group assignment, you will be required to submit your own work and words.

7. If you remain uncertain, consult the instructor.

It is important to continue to recheck the direction and focus of your work during the preparation and writing stages. Most courses will have very detailed assessment requirements, which may include marking guides or hints to help identify the correct focus or important points.

In general, markers will seek to determine whether you have:

- fully comprehended the point at issue and have kept to the topic
- argued the ideas within the word limits (if provided)
- presented your thoughts reflectively and critically (marks will generally be lost for unsupported opinion)
- shown an original and imaginative approach to the topic
- shown evidence of extensive reading and research on the topic or issue (demonstrated through in-text referencing and a list of references)
- presented your thoughts coherently and logically.

Make sure that you have clearly understood the question, and check that all required components have been answered. For example, does the question contain a descriptive or analytical element, or an element requiring your opinion and suggestions? It is possible that the assignment will contain a number of different elements. (Refer to the Resources section of this book for definitions of directive terms.)

Writing an assignment requires planning to ensure that all relevant elements have been dealt with and that the finished material is presented logically (i.e. after a suitable introduction, one idea leads to the next and finally to the conclusion). Where appropriate, make use of minor headings to help structure and focus your work. Headings help the reader follow your argument. In assignments that include headings, consider using a side heading every two or three pages and a run-in heading (set in bold and ending with a full stop, at the start of the first line of text) every three or four paragraphs. Running headings may also sometimes be useful.

Good academic writing requires not only carefully structured analysis but also a thoughtful balancing of theoretical ideas and their application to the topic. Analysis is not purely descriptive; theory should be used as a framework to support your arguments and conclusions. Similarly, students who simply provide a series of direct quotations or sections from the text without integration of these thoughts and viewpoints are unlikely to do well. Markers want to see why these views, thoughts or pieces of text are relevant to the question you are answering.

1.3 Writing guidelines

It is important to remember not to write in the same way that you speak. Conversational English is not acceptable in any formal or assessable writing. A formal style should be adopted and the use of colloquialisms or slang words and phrases, which might be acceptable in conversation, should be avoided (see figure 1.1 for examples). The reason for this is that written work, unlike the spoken word, is a permanent transcript of a writer's thoughts and ideas. The reader has time to go back over what was said and to consider how information has been presented.

Slang — to be avoided

'The experiment was a *dud*.' Not everyone knows what a 'dud' is.

'Sales *went through the roof*.' Not a very professional or informative way to say that sales increased rapidly.

Grammar/style — common errors

'It was done so as to prove the final result.' The 'so as' is not needed in this sentence. Avoid unnecessary words.

'It was *obvious* that ...' If it is obvious, you should not have to say it.

'As *said before*, the company was ...' If it has been said before, do not repeat it; alternatively, think of another way of re-emphasising the point.

Punctuation — some hints

An apostrophe 's' can mean a noun becomes possessive; that is, something belongs to it. In cases where the noun ends in any letter other than an 's' or 'x', an apostrophe followed by an 's' signifies possession (e.g. 'John's leg hurt' 'Kenwood's deep fryers were the most expensive'). If a noun already ends in an 's' or 'x' and is of one syllable, then possession is again indicated by an apostrophe 's' (e.g. 'Keats's poems', 'Marx's theories'). Exceptions to this rule include classical names (e.g. 'Mars' wrath'). In words of more than one syllable ending in an 's' or 'x', only an apostrophe is added (e.g. 'Hopkins' poems').

An apostrophe can also indicate that a letter or letters are missing from the word or that two words have been combined to make a shorter one (a contraction) — do not becomes don't (the second 'o' is removed); have not becomes haven't, and so on. A common mistake with the apostrophe is failing to distinguish between its and it's. Remember,

> *its* is possessive ('The dog loved its bone.')

> *it's* means 'it is' (the second 'i' is missing) ('It's a great day.')

FIGURE 1.1 Some common writing errors and hints

In a conversation or oral presentation, points that are unclear can be clarified immediately. In written work, this is not possible. The reader must interpret your meaning and conclusions as you have presented them, without the benefit of explanation or clarification from you, the writer. Therefore, you must choose your words carefully and provide the reader with a logical progression of thoughts and evidence that leads to the conclusion. To this end, the following points should be considered:

- Ensure the work is completed at least one day before the due date (preferably longer) to allow time for proofreading. It is often useful to give the work to someone not involved with the subject to read. If that person understands it and agrees with your conclusion, it is likely that you have produced a well-structured piece of writing. If this option is not possible, many writers find it valuable to read the report aloud (make sure no one else is around!). This helps you determine what you have really written (not what you *meant* to say) and helps to establish the natural punctuation breaks and emphases (see figure 1.1 for more hints and examples of common errors in punctuation and grammar).

- Checking spelling has been made much easier by wordprocessing software. If you are using a computer to prepare an assignment, then you should use the spellcheck function before submitting the assignment. This will not, however, pick up words that have been misused. Words often confused by students include *its* and *it's*; *affect* and *effect*; *compliment* and *complement*; *alternate* and *alternative*. There are many guides to English usage that can help. If you are not using a computerised spellchecker, a dictionary must be used to ensure no errors in spelling have occurred.

- Care must be taken to ensure that all work is free of spelling, grammatical and punctuation errors. It is inexcusable for any assessable written work to feature any of these problems.

- Slang and conversational English should be avoided (see figure 1.1).

- Be sparing in the use of adjectives and adverbs, which are often essentially value judgements.

- Many style guides recommend not using contractions (e.g. *don't*, *can't*, *haven't*) in formal writing. This recommendation applies to assignment submissions too.

- Some contractions and abbreviations do have a place in academic assignments. For example, in reference citations you may use contractions such as *eds* (for editors), *edn* (edition) and *nos* (numbers), and abbreviations such as *vol.* (for volume), *pers. comm.* (personal communication), *ver.* (version), *rev.* (revised), *n.d.* (no date). Be careful to distinguish between contractions, which include the last letter of the word and so do not take a full stop, and abbreviations, which end with a full stop to denote omitted letters at the end of the word. Established abbreviations such as 'US' (used only as an adjective) and 'ASEAN' do not require full stops.

- Use italics for emphasis very sparingly (as a rule of thumb, no more than once or twice per page). Overuse of italics reduces their impact.

- Use single quotation marks for all direct quotations except for quotes within quotes, for which double quotation marks should be used.

- Capital letters are used for the first letter in every sentence, the pronoun I and the initial letter of all proper names (i.e. the names of people, places, organisations, book titles and so on). Initial capitals should be used for a full or specific title, but lower case should be used otherwise. For example, 'The

University of Southern Queensland was one of many universities visited by Prime Minister Howard. It has been rare for prime ministers in recent years to visit regional centres ...' As a rule of thumb, if in doubt, use lower case. Also avoid using all capitals in headings; a mix of upper- and lower-case letters is easier to read.

■ Formal work should be written in the third person, using plural pronouns (e.g. use *they* instead of *he* or *she*). This will ensure that all work is perceived as objective (not a personal, unsubstantiated view) and nonsexist. Occasional use of *I* and *we* is acceptable when describing what you actually did but not to present your own value judgements (as in *I feel* ... or *I consider* ...). In report writing and case study analysis particularly, avoid using words such as *I, me, we, our, he, she*. Refer to the *Style manual* (2002, pp. 55–62) for more information.

1.3.1   Nonoffensive language

Be careful to avoid using discriminatory language. As the *Style manual* puts it:

> Linguistic discrimination can take various forms that may marginalise or exclude particular segments of the population — whether unwittingly or not. Stereotypical description of any group of people or a member of an identifiable group is probably the most insidious ... When referring to an individual, that person's sex, religion, nationality, racial group, age or physical or mental characteristics should only be mentioned if this information is pertinent to the discussion. (p. 55)

Writers should always pay particular attention to context — all writing has a context — and should be guided by discretion, tact and sensitivity in making the necessary decisions on appropriate language. Furthermore, they:

> should always bear in mind the diversity within their audiences, and ensure that references to and about particular people or social groups are couched in inclusive terms. (p. 55)

Read the *Style manual* (2002, pp. 55–62) for further guidance.

1.3.2   Use of numbers

Numbers should be expressed in figures when they accompany a symbol or unit of measurement and in tables. For example, $6.50, 9.45 am, 60 L, 9 per cent and 16 years.

When showing statistical results using percentages, the words *per cent* must be written out, except in a table, where the percentage symbol (%) should be used. For example, 'Thirty per cent of all students experience problems in referencing'.

When using numbers, the Australian standard is to use a space to separate each group of three figures in numbers greater than 999. For example, *5 000, 10 000* and *2 000 000*. Commas are not recommended to separate large numbers.

If presenting numbers smaller than one, a zero should be placed before the decimal point. For example, *0.25* and *0.67*.

Numbers below 100 are generally expressed in words; however, numbers greater than ninety-nine may also be expressed in words when the numerical expressions are used to convey approximation.

 Only a few hundred people attended the game, in spite of the 800 flyers distributed to people in the area.

Numbers that begin a sentence should be expressed in words; this also applies to years.

 Nineteen ninety-four will always be remembered . . .

If using two series of numbers in a passage, one series should be expressed as words and the other as numbers to avoid confusion.

 Twelve students scored 16 marks, and thirty students scored 24 marks.

Use numerals for parts of a document (e.g. 'chapter 3' or 'figure 6.4').

If a number includes a fraction or refers to a page number, or if there are sets of numerals, some of which are higher than ten, they should all be expressed as a number. For example, *7, 21,133*, not *seven, 21, 133*. Dates are written as *23 April 2001*; decades as *the 1970s* (not *the 1970's*); year spans as *1984–85* (not *1984–5*).

1.3.3   Tables, figures and graphs

Tables, which are generally systematic presentations of data in columns and rows, are used to clarify complicated data. Note that a marker should not have to look at tables and figures to follow your argument. Any important points made in a table or figure should be incorporated in your text. Your text should summarise the information so that a marker merely has to consult the table to check the accuracy of your interpretation. Similarly, tables and figures should be comprehensible and independent of the text, so titles and column and row headings should be self-explanatory.

All tables and figures should be numbered within the text of the assignment and have a title. They should also all be referred to in the text of the work. Tables and figures that are not referred to generally will not be considered by a marker. Tables should be placed immediately after (or as close as possible to) the paragraph containing the text referring to them. Tables that are less than a page long should not be split over a number of pages; they should start at the top of the following page. A space must always be inserted above and below a table, particularly when more than one occur on a page.

Figures are used to represent information, such as models, diagrammatically in line drawings, pictures and other illustrative forms. They can also be used to present textual information that cannot be shown logically in tabular form (i.e. in columns and rows).

All tables, figures and graphs used in assessable work must:

- have a clearly definable purpose and be referred to in the body of your work
- have a caption or title set in bold; figure and table titles should be clearly descriptive and half to three-quarters of a line long
- be numbered, and be referred to in the text by that number rather than by 'above' or 'below'
- be enclosed by a border or be in a box
- be referenced correctly when referring to another author's work, noting if adaptations have been made to the original work (see section 2.3 for referencing techniques). A source line beneath a table or figure takes the form of author or sponsoring organisation, the year in brackets and the page reference if required as when referencing for direct quotes, (e.g. *Source: Gibbs (1999, p. 63)* or *Australian Bureau of Statistics (2003)* or *Adapted from Smith & West (2005)*).

Footnotes can be used in tables to explain specific data or to provide general information relating to the data in the table.

Table, figure and graph numbering should follow paragraph numbering; that is, in chapter 2 of the document, all tables would be numbered 2.1, 2.2, 2.3 etc. in sequential order. The same principle applies to graphs and figures.

1.3.4 Titles of assessable work

The title you choose for your work, whether a report, a case study, an essay or an oral presentation, is important, because it provides the reader with a first impression and can either stimulate interest or extinguish it! Consider the following title:

> 'A study of how expenditure patterns of persons 55 years and above vary with time using a longitudinal survey consisting of household expenditure diaries distributed to a random sample of households in urban Queensland.'

It is certainly informative but it is also far too long. Ideally, you should aim for a title of about eight words. Here are some alternatives to the above:

'Expenditure of the aged' (too short and uninformative)

'A conceptualisation of a theoretical exemplar for an analysis of deviant aged expenditure' (too much jargon)

'The effect of life stage on expenditure patterns for the aged'

'A model for analysing different levels of expenditure for the aged'

The last two titles are both clearly expressed and about the right length. The appropriate choice may depend on the line of argument the writer has chosen.

In some assessments you will need to write the question or essay statement as your title.

1.3.5 Foreign terms and acronyms

Foreign terms that have not been fully absorbed into everyday English are written in italics. This does not apply to foreign terms in common use, such as *laissez faire* or *ad hoc*. If in doubt, consult a dictionary.

The first time they are used, acronyms or abbreviations should be placed in parentheses after the full name. Later references need simply use the abbreviation.

The Electoral and Administrative Review Commission (EARC) indicated in its report that ... Nevertheless, EARC went on to recommend ...

1.3.6 Parentheses

Parentheses are used to enclose expressions that are not essential to the meaning of the sentence but that amplify or clarify it, or offer an aside.

There were many at the trial who believed that Smith behaved unfairly (or so they said), whereas the outcome did not reflect this view.

Parentheses are also used to enclose letters or numbers designating a series either at the beginning of a paragraph or within a sentence, as in *(a)*, *(b)* and *(c)* or *(i)*, *(ii)* and *(iii)*.

Parentheses are also used to enclose in-text reference (author–date) information.

It is well known that whales move along the Queensland coast during the winter months to reach their breeding grounds (Smith 2006).

The punctuation used with parentheses is governed by the grammatical demands of the enclosed expression; that is, if the statement in parentheses requires a full stop, question mark or exclamation mark, then these should appear within the parentheses. A comma should be used after the parentheses only if it would have been required if the parenthetical element was not there.

The topic of his thesis (Are men really from Mars?) was controversial.

Loud applause greeted the cast (all members of the final-year student body), with the result that many felt quite emotional about the performance.

Some of the buildings that the students were studying in their architecture course had very mixed styles. (It is worth noting that this particular region is well known for the diverse mixture of architectural styles.)

Square brackets are used to enclose words or phrases inserted in quoted text by someone other than the author of the quotation.

He writes in his biography, 'Although I grew up in Darwin, I was born in Toowoomba [a large inland city two hours north of Brisbane], where my father ran a local store.'

Square brackets are also used to denote other interpolations, such as *[continued overleaf]* or *[turn to p. 44]*.

1.3.7 Points of ellipsis

The principal use of the three points of ellipsis (...) is to mark the omission of words within a quoted passage.

Every student ... must, before submitting his or her assignment, sign the declaration of original work ...

Note that only three points are used even if the ellipsis comes at the end of a sentence. No punctuation mark should precede the first point or follow the last. It is important to use marks of ellipsis when your direct quotations omit parts of the text from which you are quoting. These points indicate to the reader that the material you have quoted has been shortened for the purpose of your writing.

In creative writing, ellipses are also used to indicate faltering speech or to suggest diffidence, reluctance or irony. For example:

But ... but ... I'm sure I did it! This is the letter I spoke about a few weeks ago ...

Most of your assignment writing will use ellipses only in the former way, although for some of you who are writing up transcripts of interviews, for example, the latter situation may apply.

1.3.8 Bullet points

Use bullet points (sometimes called 'dot points') sparingly in academic writing, and only when the material in each point can be expressed as a phrase or clause ending with a semicolon or comma; that is, full sentences should not be used in bullet points. Do not indent a list of bullet points and do not leave a blank line after the introduction to the list.

Table 1.1 presents a quick guide to useful and frequently referred to pages of the *Style manual* (2002).

TABLE 1.1	Quick reference to the *Style manual*
TOPIC	**PAGE NO.**
Bulleted lists	141–4
Contractions and abbreviations	151–61
Dates	170–1
Foreign words and phrases	148–9
Harvard referencing style	188–208
Headings	137–40
Hyphens and prefixes	88–94

(Continued)

TABLE 1.1	(Continued)	
TOPIC	PAGE NO.
Inclusive communication	55–61
Names, titles and capital letters	119–35
Numbers	163–77
Points of ellipsis	110
Possessive apostrophe	85–7
Quotations	100,113–16
Tables	346–58

1.4 Presentation guidelines

When presenting written work, in addition to layout (discussed in chapters 3, 4 and 5), adhering to a number of formatting requirements will help to make your work both easier to read and easier for the marker to grade. These requirements are outlined in the following.

■ Leave a margin on all four edges of each page. Most wordprocessing programs are set up with 2.5 cm top and bottom margins and 3.2 cm left and right margins. Check the requirements of your institution.

■ The preferred font size for most submissions is 12 point. Use a proportional font such as Times New Roman.

■ Avoid using all upper-case type in text. Long passages set in upper case are difficult to read.

■ Do not use bold to emphasise or highlight words or points; instead, underline the relevant words.

■ Assignments should be typed — not handwritten — using 1½-line spacing (unless otherwise specified — some assessment layouts may require doubleline spacing). Executive summaries and lists of references should be set in single-line spacing. Leave a line space (blank line) between paragraphs and two line spaces between sections.

■ Assignments should be submitted on A4 size paper, and only one side of each page should be used.

■ Pages should be numbered in a consistent place on the page (e.g. at the top right or bottom centre of each page).

■ Each new section or subsection need not commence on a new page. However, all major headings and subheadings should be clearly identified and numbered. Make sure that headings are not left by themselves at the bottom of pages. There should be at least two lines of text under a heading at the bottom of a page. If this is not possible then move the entire section to a new page.

- Ensure that the printout is clear and easy to read. Use a new printer cartridge if possible.

- All pages should be secured with a staple in the top left-hand corner. Spiral binding is also acceptable. Do not use a paperclip or pin, because several people may need to handle the assignment before its return to you.

- Carefully proofread any assignments for typographical errors and incorrect grammar. Ask someone else to read your work to see whether it is clearly understandable and to check for errors, since your familiarity with the work reduces your ability to read it objectively.

- Check that assignments fulfil the word count requirement. The tolerance on length for most assignments is give or take 10 per cent (10 per cent more than or less than the word limit). This allowance may vary between courses, and this should be noted in the assignment instructions; if not stated, adopt the guideline given here. Be aware that some instructors may not supply any word limit. Whatever the case, extreme brevity or extreme length will be penalised. (Note that the word count should not include title page, letter of transmittal, executive summary, tables, figures, appendices or list of references.)

- Submit an original copy of the assignment and ensure that a copy is kept for your own records — if an assignment is misplaced, a copy, either electronic or in hard copy, of the original will be required.

- Ensure that you make regular backups of the work and that you generate hardcopy printouts regularly. This will allow preliminary versions of the work, or the computer disk containing the work, to be submitted to the instructor, should any last-minute computer problems be encountered. It is unlikely that last-minute extensions will be given because of computer failures without evidence of a partly completed assignment.

- Do not put assignment pages into folders that have plastic pockets for individual pages. This makes assignments difficult to process.

- If provided, use assignment cover sheets and labels for your assignment submissions.

- When submitting work electronically, ensure that you still follow standard formatting guidelines and use 'hard' page breaks to ensure that your work stays where it is supposed to be. When submitting electronically, formatting can sometimes be lost. It is also very important to make sure your title page has your name and assignment details on it and that the file name you use to save the assignment in and send it is meaningful. For example, you may save your first marketing assignment as: MKT1001Ass1Smith2009. This would allow the marker to instantly know the subject code, the assignment number and your name.

1.5 Thesis writing

Thesis writing differs from other forms of academic writing. The thesis writer should consider a number of key issues. The fundamentals of academic writing, such as use of references, use of abbreviations, numbering of tables and figures and use of capitals and punctuation, remain the same as for other forms of assessable writing. The main difference lies in the area of communication and writing style.

Communication style is of critical importance in thesis writing. While writing your thesis, consider what your examiners will be looking for; if you are fortunate enough to know who they will be, find time to read their work and study the way they communicate ideas. In this way you can discover the communication style they prefer and attempt to incorporate this into your own style.

It is important that theses are written as clearly as possible, with changes in direction clearly marked, the line of argument clearly flagged and each step explicitly explained. Most thesis examiners do not read the work in one sitting. They may pick it up and put it down many times to fit in the reading with their other commitments. It is, therefore, essential that thesis writers convey their ideas with the utmost clarity in as structured a form as possible. Do not make the examiners have to think too much, nor send them to sleep; rather, you are hoping that, even if their concentration slips at times, they can check at any time that the thesis is still on track and fulfilling the expectations set up at the start of each section and subsection. In brief, the reader needs to be guided along a smooth, easily followed path towards the conclusions that have excited the writer (Perry 2001).

Students can achieve the kind of easily followed communication essential to thesis writing by adopting four principles.

1. First, introduce new sections and subsections (each with its own descriptive bold heading) as often as every second or third page.
2. Second, start each section or subsection with a phrase or sentence linking it with what has gone before. For example, 'Given the issues discussed in section 1.4 ...' or 'Turning from international issues to domestic concerns ...' The important thing to remember is that in this way the examiners are led smoothly from the previous idea to the new one.
3. Next briefly introduce and describe at the beginning the argument or point to be made in the section. For example, 'Seven deficiencies in models in the literature will be identified ...' Make each step in the argument easy to follow and identify with a key term in italics or the judicious use of point enumeration (*first, second*) or linking words (*moreover, in addition* and so on).
4. Finally, end each section with a summary to establish what it has achieved. This summary sentence or paragraph can be flagged by beginning 'In conclusion ...' or 'In brief ...'

These four principles will make your arguments easier to follow and so encourage the examiners towards accepting your views.

The thesis is essentially a long piece of work that develops an idea or concept in depth. It is important that each part of it is carefully considered in terms of its role in the exposition. Each 'chunk', or idea, within the thesis needs to be carefully linked to the other chunks to give continuity to the whole document. Within this concept of chunks and links, think about the role of the paragraph and the sentence. Each paragraph deals with one idea that is introduced in a theme sentence near the start. The start of a paragraph is a 'hot spot' that every reader will focus on (Lindsay 1995). By contrast, each sentence contains one small idea, with the most important part of the sentence presented at the start. Do not waste the 'hot spot' at the start of a sentence or paragraph on unimportant information such as, 'As shown in table 6.1 ...' or 'Smagers & Brown (1998) state ...' Place this sort of reference information at the end of the sentence and use the prime space to communicate a clear idea to the reader. In brief, the thesis should consist of a string of clear chunks of ideas that are well linked in a storyline that is easy to follow and understand.

For further information on thesis writing in particular, refer to: Perry, C 1998, 'A structured approach to presenting theses', *Australasian Marketing Journal*, vol. 6, no. 1, pp. 63-85.

1.6 Making the most of the library

1.6.1 What is in the library?

University libraries hold vast numbers of books and thousands of journal titles as well as maps, videos, CD-ROM databases, music cassettes and CDs. Access to databases holding all material is through the library's electronic catalogue. The library is your most important resource as a student.

1.6.2 Finding your way in the library

Most libraries conduct tours to familiarise students with their layout and operation. You are encouraged to attend one of these. Most libraries also conduct classes on how to go about finding information for assignments. Check your individual libraries for times and dates.

Libraries usually hold collections of videos and computer-aided learning packages, which will help you learn how to use the library and to research assignments. Look for handouts produced by the library staff on how to research subjects, use databases, reference citations and other useful topics.

1.6.3 Ways to access information

How information is accessed is rapidly changing. Print materials are now complemented by databases on CD-ROMs and on-line. These can help you find references to journal articles and, in the case of full-text databases, the articles themselves. There are multimedia CDs offering graphics, text, sound and animation. Libraries also subscribe to electronic databases, which can be accessed through their electronic gateways; many sites on the Internet provide a wealth of information. However, newest is not always best, so do not always rely on just one source of information (e.g. using only CD-ROM databases when there might be superior paper indices).

1.7 Summary

When preparing written work for assessment or review, it is important that students:

- understand and answer each of the questions posed in the assessment specifications
- start work on the assignment as soon as possible (avoid the temptation to procrastinate)
- use the resources provided in the library, in their texts and on-line to the greatest extent possible to research the topic or topics
- ensure that their work is presented in accordance with general good practice requirements and the specific requirements of the marker
- ensure that numbers, tables, figures and graphs are presented in a consistent manner and according to the guidelines outlined in this handbook

- proofread their work at least once (preferably more than once) before submission to remove errors such as incorrect punctuation, poor grammar and incorrect spelling

- ensure that they have adequately and correctly referenced any information taken from other sources (including the Internet) — failure to adopt this practice is likely to result in allegations of plagiarism and academic misconduct

- ensure that slang words and phrases, conversational English and offensive language are not used.

This chapter has presented hints and guidelines relating to each of the preceding points. Having followed the guidelines presented, students must also cite sources of information included in their work. The next chapter discusses one method for achieving this.

2 Referencing

2.1 Introduction

A vital skill that all university students should develop is the ability to evaluate existing knowledge critically and, in so doing, further develop their own understanding of an area of study. Students are often required to demonstrate this ability by producing a written document, such as an essay or report, that interweaves their own ideas and arguments with ideas and arguments documented by other authors.

For your work to have depth and credibility, you must demonstrate having read widely on the topic by including information from a range of sources. However, it is important for the reader of the work to know which information in the document has been developed by you, the author, and which information you have borrowed from others. Referencing allows the reader to locate your original source material.

The purpose of referencing in written work is to:

- allow readers of the document to find the original source and learn more about some aspect that the author may have mentioned only briefly in the document

- properly record information sources so that the author can find the original sources of the information used to develop the document should he or she choose to do so at a later time

- provide theoretical support or evidence for statements or conclusions made by the writer

- acknowledge the intellectual property of others and thus avoid the possibility of the author being accused of plagiarism.

Unethical behaviour is discussed in the following section. The chapter then introduces referencing and goes on to provide many practical examples of the Harvard referencing style.

2.2 Unethical behaviour

2.2.1 Plagiarism[1]

The practice of using another writer's ideas or observations and presenting them as your own is called plagiarism. Academic writers are expected to be especially vigilant in this regard. Examples of plagiarism include:

- when blocks of text (e.g. paragraphs, sentences, a single sentence or a significant part of a single sentence) are copied directly but are not enclosed in quotation marks and appropriately referenced

---

1 The contribution to the development of this section on plagiarism by Dr Lesley Willcoxon is gratefully acknowledged.

- when direct quotations are not used but material is paraphrased or summarised in such a way that it substantially reflects ideas taken from another author's work, and the source of the material is not appropriately referenced
- when an idea that appears in printed or electronic form has been used or developed without reference being made to the person responsible for that idea.

If you directly quote an author's words, you must acknowledge that these are not your words by using quotation marks and giving the author's name, date of publication and page number. If you do not acknowledge the original source of the words, you are committing plagiarism.

Not plagiarism
'Human resource planning is important because an organisation's effectiveness depends on having the right people in the right jobs at the right times' (Stone 2008, p. 49). If an organisation does not . . .

Plagiarism
Human resource planning is important because an organisation's effectiveness depends on having the right people in the right jobs at the right times. If an organisation does not . . .

If what you say is almost the same as what the author said but you have changed a few words, you must acknowledge that these are basically someone else's words by giving the author's name and the date of publication. This is called paraphrasing. If you do not acknowledge the original source of the words, you are guilty of plagiarism.

Not plagiarism
Human resource planning is important because if organisations do not have the best people in appropriate jobs at a time when they are needed then they are likely to have serious shortfalls (Stone 2008).

Plagiarism
Human resource planning is important because organisations need to have appropriate people in appropriate jobs at a time when they are needed. If organisations do not ...

If you use someone else's ideas, you must acknowledge that these are not your own original ideas by giving the author's name and the date of publication of the source material. In the case that follows, Stone makes the same point in several places throughout the book so it is not necessary to provide a specific page number. However, if you were to use Stone's exact words and phrasing then you must consider this to be a direct quote. If you do not acknowledge the original source of ideas you have used in your assignment work, you will be found guilty of plagiarism.

Not plagiarism
If organisations are to function as well as possible, they need to make sure that staff are available to fill jobs when the need arises (Stone 2008). If they do not ensure this ...

As Stone (2008) states, if organisations are to function as well as possible, they need to make sure that staff are available to fill jobs when the need arises. If they do not ensure this ...

Plagiarism
If organisations are to function as well as possible, they need to make sure that staff are available to fill jobs when the need arises. If they do not ensure this ...

Plagiarism is cheating and is totally unacceptable in university work. In written work submitted for assessment in most universities, plagiarism may lead not only to assignment failure but also to serious formal proceedings under the university's academic regulations (see your student rulebook).

2.2.2 Collusion

The practice of working in groups to share ideas, either formally or informally, is accepted and encouraged as an approach to learning in university study. However, all assignments must be submitted individually unless students are specifically directed otherwise. It is *not* acceptable, unless otherwise clearly stipulated in writing by the course examiner, for two or more students to submit identical work or to submit copies of work done as a group. Examiners are entitled to consider identical layout, identical mistakes, identical argument and identical presentation as prima facie evidence of collusion. It is also important that you protect your work from intentional and unintentional copying by other students. You must ensure that your electronic copies of assignments are not able to be viewed by other students before the submission deadlines. Cases where students have provided their work knowingly to other students either in hardcopy or electronic form before submission are also considered to be acts of collusion and both students are likely to be heavily penalised.

In general, it is critical that students have a very clear understanding of the submission requirements of each course by carefully reading the instructions and that they take all measures to avoid allegations of collusion.

2.3 Referencing — general information

2.3.1 When to provide a reference

A reference is required in the following instances:

- *Direct quotation*. When another writer's work is quoted verbatim (word for word). Whether a phrase, sentence or paragraph, the quote must be enclosed in single quotation marks and a reference to the source provided.

- *Paraphrasing or summarising*. Ideas or data obtained from another writer must be referenced — *even if the wording or context has been changed*.

- *Controversial information, opinions or data that an informed reader might challenge*. If, for example, an author states that Australia was first discovered by Europeans in 1522 (instead of much later, as is commonly accepted), the author will have to support that assertion by acknowledging the source of the information.

- *Tables, figures, diagrams and appendices*. When statistical data, diagrams or illustrations are either taken whole or adapted from another source, that source must be cited.

In short, students must reference any ideas or data that are not their own. Information of a general nature, such as facts and ideas that are common knowledge, do not need references. For example, that the Commonwealth of Australia was created in 1901 is well known and undisputed, so no reference is required in this case. If at any stage in your work a reader might ask the question, 'How does the writer know this information?' or 'Where did they get this idea from?', then you can be confident that a reference or citation is required.

2.3.2 Referencing — a helpful hint

 It is always much easier to record the complete and correct reference for sources used in works at the time the information is first found. Therefore, when making photocopies of information to be used in assignments, always ensure that *at the time of photocopying*, you collect *all the source information* you will require to cite the source properly. The best way to do this is either to photocopy the title and copyright pages of the book or journal containing the article, or to simply handwrite the relevant information on the photocopy. Furthermore, when transcribing or using information from a source, you should get into the habit of inserting the complete reference *at the time the information is transcribed or viewed*. Trying to find the necessary information later can be a frustrating task. Be particularly careful to take this information when using electronic sources as websites can change and you may never be able to locate that particular article or piece of information again without the exact electronic reference. Make sure you also note the date and time you sourced the information as this will protect you if the information is no longer electronically available, this information shows when it was available and allows future tracking.

Remember, also, that when you are using references and quotations to support your discussion in written work, you must summarise in your own words the significance of the quotation and how it adds to, or supports, your argument or view. You need to show the reader that you have understood the meaning of the referenced work; you should not leave it for the reader to try to work out how the reference or quotation relates to your discussion. It is likely that students who submit work that comprises a series of direct quotations without any integration, discussion or application to the assignment topic or question will receive poor results.

2.4 Methods of referencing

The primary purpose of referencing is to enable the reader to locate the source of material taken from another author's work easily. Therefore, it is important, first, that the author provides the reader with all *relevant information* for each source and, second, that the information is presented in a *consistent format* throughout the document.

Information published using traditional paper-based methods is static once printed and is, therefore, relatively easy to cite. Many methods of referencing have been developed to facilitate a standard approach to the task. Commonly used methods include the Harvard system (also known as the author–date system), the Chicago system (also known as the footnoting system) and the Vancouver system, although many other systems are in use. This guide will focus on examples using the Harvard system.

Some methods are preferred, and in some cases mandated, by various disciplines but are not favoured by others. Occasionally, even journals within the same discipline may use conflicting referencing methods.

The recent rise in electronic publishing has made the task of appropriately referencing sources of information more complex. Information that must be recorded about electronically published material differs from that required for paper-based material. This is mainly because of the different ways that electronic information is represented and accessed compared with traditional methods. Information published in electronic form has the potential to be highly dynamic. First, in the case of Internet sources, information may change from day to day, or even minute to minute. Information available to someone accessing a particular site at 9.00 am may differ greatly from information available from the same site at 10.00 pm on the same day. Second, the location of information is also subject to change.

Because computers require precision, the author must take particular care to ensure that the names of Internet sites are recorded accurately, in terms of both spelling and capitalisation. Standards for citing electronic material are still developing but a section describing the current required approach to referencing electronic material has been included later in this chapter.

Rules and examples pertaining to presentation of in-text references and lists of references are included in the following sections.

The explanations and examples provided cover the commonly occurring situations only, and are therefore not exhaustive. For a more detailed introduction to referencing, students should refer to chapter 12 of the *Style manual* (2002).

2.5 The Harvard system

Authors using the Harvard system must include both of the following for each citation:

- an in-text reference (acknowledgement in the main body of the document)
- a corresponding entry in the list of references (LOR; a list of all the sources cited in the report, with the exception of personal communications).

2.6 In-text references

This section describes how to insert references in the body of the text using the Harvard referencing system.

2.6.1 Format

An in-text reference includes:

- the surname(s) of the author(s) of the work
- the year the work was published (where appropriate)
- the page number(s) where the cited information can be found in the publication.

Note: A page number is required if you are referring to a direct quotation or to figures/data produced in a research project.

In general, it is advisable not to begin a sentence or paragraph with a citation to authorities.

Avoid

Smith, Brown, Adams and Zikopoelus (2009) suggested that marketing is the key functional area of any business.

Better

In a recent research report by Smith, Brown, Adams and Zikopoelus (2009), it was suggested that marketing is the key functional area of any business.

Best

Marketing is the key functional area of any business (Smith, Brown, Adams & Zikopoelus 2009).

The year and page number(s), when provided, are always enclosed within parentheses. The name of the author(s) may or may not be enclosed in parentheses depending on the circumstance (see preceding examples). Specific in-text referencing rules and examples (citing paper-based sources) follow.

2.6.2 When to include page numbers

The page number must be included in the reference when directly quoting a block of text or when including statistical data from a source. Page numbers are not usually necessary (check your specific assignment instructions) when paraphrasing or borrowing a general theme or idea from a work. If you are taking text directly from the Internet you also need to include the page number which should be evident in the electronic reference (see the section on electronic referencing).

When including page numbers, the correct format for one page is 'p. 6'. For two or more pages 'pp. 23–37' should be used (*Style manual* 2002, p. 194). Page numbers should indicate where the quote starts and finishes. If the start and finish page numbers are in the same decimal range (e.g. 20 and 29, or 322 and 328), the finishing page number should include only the relevant final digits of the number (e.g. 20–9 or 322–8).

In cases in which quotes run over nonconsecutive pages, 'pp.' should be used and the page numbers should be separated by a comma. The following examples illustrate the use of page numbers.

(Wells 2009, p. 4) — note the position of the comma after the year and a space before the p.

(Smith 2008, pp. 1, 4, 6) — i.e. pages 1, 4 and 6

(Jones & Mackey 2009, pp. 25–6) — i.e. pages 25 to 26

(Arbut, King & Browning 2009, pp. 459–87) — i.e. pages 459 to 487

2.6.3 Footnotes

Although footnotes are permitted in the Harvard system, they are not used for citing sources. Footnotes may be used for providing information that is incidental to the main argument in the text. For example, a footnote could be used to expand on or explain a term or a point raised that is relevant but if included in the main body of the text, would interrupt the flow of the discourse. Terms such as *op. cit.*, *ibid.* and *id.* are not used in the Harvard system.

2.6.4   Short quotations

Direct quotes should be enclosed in *single* quotation marks. If the quote does not begin at the start of a sentence, the author should use three dots (an ellipsis) to convey this to the reader. Ellipses should also be used to indicate when the remainder of a sentence quoted is not included. See section 1.3.7 for more information on ellipses and the following pages for examples.

2.6.5   Long quotations

Where direct quotes exceed 30 words they should be indented from the left margin and single line spaced *without* quotation marks. The quote should be introduced by a colon (:) and one line space should separate the quote from the introductory statement and from the text that follows. The quote should be set one point size smaller than the font used for the main text (*Style manual* 2002, p. 113). See section 2.6.6 for an example.

2.6.6   Single author

The following examples show how to include in-text references for sources with one author.

The population of Amitamia in 2008 was 17.6 million (Hogg 2002, p. 35).

Johnson (2007, p. 27) stated that '... lack of exercise is our most serious problem'. Note the quote has not taken all of the information from this author and the ellipses indicate that the sentence is only quoted in part and that the first part is missing.

The incidence of coronary disease in Australian males has increased in the past ten years (Williams 2009).

Tanenbaum (2008, p. 1) has the following to say about technological evolution:

> Each of the past three centuries has been dominated by a single technology. The 18th Century was the time of great mechanical systems accompanying the Industrial Revolution. The 19th Century was the age of the steam engine. During the 20th Century, the key technology has been information gathering, processing and distribution.

2.6.7   Two or more authors

When a work has two authors, *both* names should be included in every citation (*Style manual* 2002); the authors' names should be separated by an ampersand (&) if enclosed in parentheses or separated by *and* if the names are outside the parentheses (see the examples that follow). Where three or more authors are cited, the same format applies except that the first two (or more) names are separated by a comma and only the last two are separated by &.

Where there are more than three authors, the in-text references can be abbreviated to improve the readability of the text and only the first author's name need be included followed by *et al.* (meaning 'and others'). In cases where there are different combinations of authors with the same first author, enough of the author names should be used in citations to avoid confusion. All authors' surnames should be used in the LOR.

Initials should be used in the citations only in situations where two different authors share the same surname.

It has been recently revealed that zebras are not native to Africa (Hichell & Williams, P 2007). . . . Hichell and Williams, P (2008) now contend that zebras originated in Iceland. Other authors dispute this statement (Williams, H 2009).

Here two authors share the surname Williams and the use of initials allows the reader to differentiate between them.

Network technologies have become increasingly complex in recent times (Cook, Burger & Brown 2009). . . . Local area networks are now very common (Samson et al. 2009).

Here (*Samson et al. 2009*) refers to a 2009 publication by Samson, Thames, Burger, Brown and Cook.

2.6.8 Two or more works in one citation

When two or more works are included in one citation, they should be arranged in alphabetical order and delimited by a semicolon.

The decrease in the zebra population appears to be related to an increase in technological innovation (Cook, Burger & Brown 2008; Hichell & Williams 2008).

When two or more works from the same author are cited, they should be listed in chronological order.

The zebra population in Africa is declining (Hichell & Williams 2007, 2008, 2009).

When two or more works from the same author in the same year are cited, append *a*, *b*, *c* and so on to the year. This should reflect the order presented in the LOR.

Local area networks are used by more and more organisations (Bruin 2008a, 2008b).

2.6.9 Newspapers

Newspapers should be cited as shown in the following examples (note the use of italics and omission of *The* from the newspaper title).

The following example shows how a newspaper article whose author is not known should include all details in the in-text citation. In this case, no entry is required in the LOR (*Style manual* 2002, p. 206), as follows:

A new American president has been elected (*Weekend Australian* 24–25 February 2009) ... In the *Financial Review* (25 July 2008, p. 23).

If the author of the article is known, then the author–year format should be used, and the full reference provided in the LOR.

A new American president has been elected (Bloggs 2009).

For frequent references to the same newspaper material, abbreviations are acceptable. For example, the *Sydney Morning Herald* is shortened to *SMH*.

2.6.10 Personal communications

A corresponding entry in the LOR is not required for personal communications, since they cannot be retrieved by the reader. However, the person's surname, initials, *pers. comm.* and the date of the communication must be included in the text. You must also be sure to obtain permission from the person being referred to. Note that the initials of the person *precede* the family name.

A survey is currently being undertaken by John Smith to ascertain the acceptance of electronic payment methods in the community (J Smith 2008, pers. comm., 15 May).

When interviewed on 22 September, Mr P Frank admitted that the major problems for Telstra's marketing division were coming from the organisation's recent expansion. Mr P Frank (Telstra marketing manager) confirmed the press rumours by facsimile on 15 May 2008.

This is also the format used for email communications, although you should be careful to verify the source of the email communication before citing it as a personal communication.

Note: Students should not quote statements made by lecturers or tutors unless the information quoted has been officially published. External study guides and notes are considered by most universities to be official publications, and any material taken from them must be acknowledged.

2.6.11 Anonymous works

In cases where the author's name is not available, *anonymous* should not be used. Either the sponsoring organisation (see section 2.6.13) or the title of the article (in italics) should be included. When determining the alphabetical order of these references, ignore words at the start of the title such as *a*, *an* or *the*.

Large numbers of organisations are now using the Internet as a marketing tool (*The web as a marketing tool* 2008).

2.6.12 Publication date unavailable

If the publication date of a source cannot be ascertained, *n.d.* may be used or, where it is possible to approximate the date of publication, *c.* (from the Latin circa, meaning *about*) may be used.

It seems that technology has encouraged people to lead sedentary lives (Moorbent n.d.). Althaus (c. 2008, p. 2) supported this assertion and stated that '... in today's society ... because of computers'.

2.6.13 Sponsoring organisation

When there is no specific author but the name of the organisation sponsoring the publication is available, the organisation's name should be included.

In a publication by the University of Southern Queensland (2007), the Vice Chancellor said ...

In a recent report it was stated that '... raging dry season bushfires are easily the most dramatic feature of the Australian scene' (Department of Primary Industries 2007, p. 56).

2.6.14 Unpublished works

When students cite an unpublished source, such as a letter, minutes of a meeting or a company report, the in-text reference guidelines are the same as for journals and periodicals. That is, the author or sponsoring organisation, and the year of publication (if known) are included. Other in-text referencing rules apply if no publication date is available (see section 2.6.12), the work is anonymous (see section 2.6.11) or more than one work by the same author is cited (see section 2.6.8).

The changes to the structure of the organisation were not only planned, but also strategically motivated as evidenced in the intercompany fax between the managing director and the union representative (Harrison 2007).

It was evident from the minutes of the July meeting (National Teachers Union 2007) that many teachers were unaware of the implications of the decision to accept the changes proposed by the federal government.

2.6.15 Citations for sources other than the original

Books of readings

In the case of material taken from a book of readings, students are required to inform the reader that the material cited is not taken from the original source. This should be done through an appropriate entry in the LOR (see section 2.7.4 for further explanation). The in-text citation references the original source of the material as shown in the following.

Stallings and Van Slyke (in Cappel 2008) defined a digital signal as '... a sequence of voltage pulses that may be transmitted over a wire medium'.

Indirect quotations

In general, students must make every attempt to discover the original source of a quotation. However, there may be instances when the original source is inaccessible for some reason (e.g. it is out of print) or the original source is in a foreign language. In these cases it is permissible to use an indirect quote from another source. The original author, year of publication and page number(s) (where appropriate) should be quoted in the in-text reference in the normal manner. However, both the original source and the indirect source should be included in the LOR entry and should be separated by the words 'cited in' to acknowledge that an indirect quotation has been used (see section 2.7 for an example of the LOR entry).

2.6.16 Tables and figures either extracted or taken whole

When tables or figures are extracted or presented in their entirety in documents, the reference should:

- be presented using the same format as that used in an LOR for that type of source
- be preceded by *Source:*
- be enclosed in parentheses
- include the page number(s) preceded by *p.* or *pp.* as appropriate.

The following example shows a table taken in its entirety from a *book*:

Animal	Population (1990)	Population (1995)	Population (2000)
Zebra	300 000	270 000	250 000
Lion	60 000	65 000	68 000

(*Source:* Edwards et al. 2008, p. 67)

If some parts of the table were taken from another author's work but other parts were added (e.g. a column or row was added to the table or only part of the table included), then the word *Source:* should be replaced by *Adapted from:* and the reference or references for multiple sources provided.

2.7 LOR entries for paper-based sources — specific rules and examples

Authors using the Harvard system must include in-text references *and* either an LOR or a bibliography. In both an LOR and a bibliography, publications are listed in *alphabetical order* based on authors' surnames. Multiple references to the same author should be listed in chronological order.

An LOR differs from a bibliography in the following way: only sources actually *cited* in the main body of the text are included in an LOR. All references used in the preparation of the document, whether or not they are cited, are listed in a bibliography.

Unless specifically directed by their course examiner to do otherwise, students are advised to include an LOR with written work; that is, only sources actually cited in the work should be included.

Titles of books and articles should be listed using minimal capitalisation. The original title, as used on the cover, should be preserved in the reference.

Full stops and spaces are not used with initials, and book and periodical names are italicised. Commas are used to separate items.

Each listing should be separated by a space. Examples of how to include commonly occurring items in an LOR are provided in the following pages.

2.7.1 LOR — book citation

The general format for including a book entry in an LOR is as follows:

<Author's surname>, <Author's initial(s) — no spaces between initials if more than one> <year of publication>, in <editor, reviser, compiler or translator if applicable>, *<Title of publication>*, <edition abbreviated as edn, e.g. 2nd edn>, <volume number if applicable, abbreviated as vol.>, <publisher>, <place of publication>, <page number if applicable>.

The title of the publication is italicised. Where there are two authors, the names are separated by &. For more than two authors, all surnames are separated by a comma, other than the final two, which are separated by an ampersand (&). The abbreviation *ed.* is used to indicate one editor, and *eds* is used to indicate more than one editor. Edition is abbreviated to *edn*.

Brady, J 2008, *International marketing*, Prentice Hall, Toronto.

Michael, F & Emming, BM 2009, *Strategic planning*, 5th edn, Prentice Hall, London.

Cranbourne, CA, Keane, B & Sumner, CC 2008, *African wildlife*, Irwin, Chicago.

Campbell, HB (ed.) 2009, *Internet information sources*, Pergamon Press, Oxford.

2.7.2 LOR — article or chapter in an edited book

The same format is used here as for the preceding, except that the author of the chapter or article is acknowledged first, the title of the article or chapter is enclosed in single quotation marks, and the editors are included before the title of the book. It should also be noted that the editors' initials precede their surname. The word 'in' is also included to indicate that the chapter is contained within a book and is not the title of the book.

Axelsson, B & Easton, G 2009, 'Foreign market entry — the textbook vs the network theory', in B Axelsson & G Easton (eds), *Industrial networks: a new view of reality*, Routledge, London, pp. 46–59.

2.7.3 LOR — lecture notes/study notes

Lecture notes, study notes or course material provided by your lecturer should be listed in the same manner as a book.

Smith, B 2008, *Networks and distributed systems study book*, Distance Education Centre, USQ, Toowoomba, Australia.

Smith, B 2008, CIS1000 *Information Systems for Managers: 2008 lecture notes 6th September 2008*, University of Southern Queensland, Semester 2, 2008.

The following format applies where the author's name is not known:

Networks and distributed systems study book 2008, Distance Education Centre, USQ, Toowoomba, Australia.

2.7.4 LOR — books of readings

In the case of books of readings, students are required to include both a reference to the original article and a reference to the book of readings from which the article was sourced, as shown in the example that follows. This will allow the reader to obtain the material from either source.

Stallings, W & Van Slyke, R 2008, 'Signal encoding', *Business data communications*, 2nd edn, Prentice Hall, New Jersey, p. 28, cited in B Smith (ed.) 2008, *Networks and distributed systems selected readings*, Distance Education Centre, USQ, Toowoomba, Australia, reading 3.1.

2.7.5 LOR — indirect quotation

When a source is quoted in the text but that source is not the original source of the quotation, the following format should be used:

Galvin, P 2009, *Electronic principles*, cited in Stallings, W & Van Slyke, R 2009, 'Signal encoding', *Business data communications*, 2nd edn, Macmillan College Publishing Company Inc., New York, p. 23.

2.7.6 LOR — article in journal

Articles require the same basic format as books, except that the title of the article is enclosed in single quotes, a volume number (abbreviated to vol.) and series number (abbreviated to no.) for the journal are included and page numbers are added. Sometimes a series number is not available but a season such as *Autumn* or *Summer* or a period such as March/May may be used instead.

Major, A, Ng, DG & Barr, NW 2007, 'A proposition-based approach to a market exit strategy', *Journal of International Marketing*, vol. 3, no. 5, pp. 69–87.

Dennis, R 2007, 'Theory and practice in marketing research', *Journal of Marketing*, vol. 27, Summer, pp. 131–40.

Andresson, H & Crewes, LP 2008, 'International market channels of distribution', *Journal of Marketing*, vol. 34, January, pp. 71–82.

2.7.7 LOR — sponsoring organisation

Sometimes a specific author is not known. In this case the sponsoring organisation may be used.

Bureau of Transport Economics 2008, *Economic regulations of aviation in Australia*, seminar papers and proceedings, AGPS, Canberra.

Austrade 2009, 'Exporting of services comes into focus', *Business Review Weekly*, 17 September, p. 1.

2.7.8 LOR — multiple publications by the same author

Where several works by the same author are listed, the author's name may be replaced by a two-em rule (see *Style manual* 2002, pp. 194–5) in the second and subsequent entries in the LOR. For works by the same author in the same year, an alphabetic suffix is appended to the year (e.g. *1999a, 1999b*).

Sheridan, G 2008, 'Children and education', *Courier-Mail*, 3 March, p. 2.

—— 2008a, 'Early childhood learning', *Weekend Australian*, 4 August, p. 5.

—— 2008b, 'Our youngsters', *Weekend Australian*, 4 December, p. 7.

—— & Smith, L 2007, 'The education system exposed', *Business Review Weekly*, 4 January, p. 5.

2.7.9 LOR — conference paper, working paper series and thesis

For papers presented to conferences but not published in proceedings, the correct format is as follows:

Ritchie, JB 2008, 'Accessing international education markets', paper presented to 3rd Internationalising Education Conference, Sydney, 22–23 September.

For papers presented at a conference and published in conference proceedings, the format is as follows:

DuPont, B 2008, 'Marketing and the Internet: implications for managers', *Proceedings of the third annual Australian Marketing Association*, Melbourne, Australian Marketing Association, Melbourne, Australia, pp. 44–6.

Working paper series:

Selvarajah, CT 2008, 'Marketing education in Malaysia: implications for Australian tertiary institutions', *Faculty of Business & Commerce staff papers*, working paper no. 43, Swinburne Institute of Technology, Melbourne.

Theses:

Crowley, FK 2008, 'Working class conditions in Australia, 1788–1851', PhD thesis, University of Melbourne.

Naudi, A 2000, 'Change management', MIT thesis, University of Southern Queensland.

2.7.10 LOR — article in newspaper or magazine

The format for newspaper or magazine articles is very similar to that used for journals.

Austrade 2008, 'Exporting of services comes into focus', *Business Review Weekly*, 17 September, p. 1.

Keating, P 2009, 'The "quiet revolution"', *Asian Business Review*, April, pp. 16–17.

The New Straits Times 2009, 'One more time', 24 January, p. 32.

2.7.11 LOR — unpublished works

For unpublished works, such as papers presented at seminars, manuscripts, letters, faxes and reports, the following guidelines apply for the LOR. (Unpublished electronic works such as emails are addressed in section 2.9.7.) The author's name and the year of preparation of the document are presented in the manner described for articles in journals and periodicals. The title of the work (if appropriate) should also be presented in the same manner but without quotation marks. Other details should be provided with a view to guiding the reader as efficiently as possible. These details will vary according to the nature of the document. Personal communications need not be included in lists of references but are cited in the text itself.

Harrison, Q 2008, planning requirements for restructure, Brisbane Chamber of Commerce and Industry, fax to J Golding, 24 July.

Cranbourne, F 2009, Western Computer Supplies, letter to G Wilson, Queensland secretary, Australian Manufacturing Workers Union, 24 April.

Insurance Council of Australia 2008, submission to the Committee of Inquiry into Workers Compensation in Victoria, workers compensation report, Melbourne, 19 December.

National Teachers Union, Brisbane Branch 2008, minutes of branch committee meeting, Brisbane, 2 June.

2.8 Electronic referencing method

Traditional paper-based referencing methods are not adequate for appropriately citing works that have been published using electronic methods. A number of scholars have proposed methods for referencing electronic documents (Li & Crane 1993, 1996; *Electronic sources: APA style of citation* n.d.; *Electronic sources: MLA style of citation* n.d.; Lamp n.d.; Page 1996) and the *Style manual* (2002) also deals with the issue on pages 230–1.

It is important for students to maintain as much consistency as possible between the referencing system used for paper-based works and that used for electronic works. There are a number of methods that follow either APA (American Psychological Association) or MLA (Modern Language Association) style. Here, the focus is on those based on the Harvard format.

2.8.1 Electronic referencing — general information

As previously described for paper-based referencing (see section 2.4), two components are required when referencing electronic sources of information; namely, an in-text reference and a corresponding entry in the LOR at the end of the document.

2.8.2 In-text references — electronic sources

When referencing electronic information, the Harvard format should be used for in-text references. The name of the author, or the title of the article, or the name of the sponsoring organisation (if the author is unknown), should be included along with the year and the relevant page numbers, if applicable. If citing a URL, the date of the last update should be given. The use of angle brackets (< >) around the URL is recommended.

When the author is known and the page numbers are relevant the in-text reference follows that of a traditional paper-based reference:

People are now living longer than they did a century ago (Brown 2008). This finding has been further supported by Smith (2009, p. 4), who stated that . . .

When the author is unknown and the sponsoring organisation is relevant:

As a direct result of pollution, vegetation is dying on the hillsides (Australian Conservation Foundation 2008).

When the author is unknown and a URL is provided (*note:* rather than a year, the last date the site was updated is given if known):

Sporting events now constitute 9 out of 10 most watched television programs in American history (<www.baysider.com/Features/superbowl.html>, March 2008).

2.8.3 LOR — electronic sources, general

Generally speaking, entries in the LOR should follow the Harvard system (see sections 2.6 and 2.7). However, owing to the dynamic nature of electronic publishing, additional information must be included when citing references for works published using this medium.

If the information was obtained from the Internet, the address of the site where the information was stored (in angled brackets < >) and the date when the information was accessed (prefixed by 'viewed') should be included. This warns the reader that the information or facts and figures included in the text by the author were current on the stated site on the date it was accessed by the author but that changes in the content or location of the information may have occurred since that date.

Some examples are included in the following to illustrate how different types of electronic material should be cited.

2.9 LOR entries for electronic sources — specific rules and examples

2.9.1 CD-ROM — book/electronic books

Note that Microsoft is the producer of the CD-ROM in the first example that follows, and that the date is the date of production of the CD-ROM. The date of access is not required for a CD-ROM because, similarly to paper-based material, the information on any particular edition will not change after it has been published.

Clark, MK 2008, *Birds of Australia*, CD-ROM, 2nd edn, Microsoft Corporation.

'The American Presidents' 2009, in *The 2009 Grolier Multimedia Encyclopedia*, CD-ROM, ver. 7, Grolier Inc., 2009.

Marks, J & Stephens, P 2007, *A Guide to Flower Arranging*, Prentice Hall, New Jersey, Viewed 17 January 2009, http://bartleby.com/117/.

2.9.2 Electronic journal articles

Wallace, B 2007, 'Microwave, infrared products target LANs', *Computerworld*, vol. 31, no. 4, p. 56, viewed 20 March 2009, EBSCOhost MegaFILE Premier, Academic Search Premier item: AN589758.

Anderson, H 2006, 'Turning intranets into strategic marketing weapons', *Network World*, vol. 14, no. 4, p. 4, viewed 20 March 2003, EBSCOhost database, Business Source Elite, item:01363555.

Note that *item* in these examples refers to the accession number of the article on the database. This number is an index and provides fast access to the document when using the database. Also note that you need to provide the date the database was viewed.

For journal articles on the web.

Griffiths, M 2007, 'Gaining the attention of Gen Y with Marketing Communications', *Journal of Marketing Research*, vol. 3, no. 2, viewed 21 January 2009, http://JMR.edu.com/pass/0980-lt.

If no author is provided.

Economist 2008, 'The future looks bleak!', vol. 45, no. 24, p. 53, viewed 8 February 2009, EBSCOhost Megafile Premier, Australia/new Zealand Reference Center, item: 457891.

2.9.3 Internet sites (author and date available)

Lee, MT 2007, *Guidelines for citing references and electronic sources of information*, viewed 12 May 2008, <www.eliz.tased.edu.au/refs.htm>.

Note that the address of the website must be included and preceded by 'viewed'. Care must be taken to ensure that the capitalisation and spelling of the address of the site is preserved exactly.

2.9.4 Internet sites (author and date not available)

Guidelines for citing references and electronic sources of information n.d., viewed 12 May 2008, <www.eliz.tased.edu.au/refs.htm>.

The Body Shop Australia 2008, The Body Shop Australia, Victoria, Viewed 5 January 2009, <http://www.thebodyshop.com.au>

2.9.5 Newspaper articles

Referencing electronically available newspaper articles follow the same conventions as traditional paper based ones.

Author Year, 'Article title', *Newspaper title*, Day Month, page number (if known), viewed Day Month Year, <URL>.

Kayle, W 2009, 'It's a long way to the top, if you are a bank manager', *The Weekend Australian*, 14 February, viewed 3 March 2009, <http://www. theaustralian.news.com.au/story/0,25197,25262346-12377,00.html>.

2.9.6 Discussion group messages/Weblogs/Wikis and podcasts

The general format for citing a discussion list message is as follows:

<Author> <Author's identifying details — usually email address> <Date when message was posted>, <Title of posting>, <Discussion Group Name>, <Discussion group owner>, <Date of viewing>, <URL>.

Brown, F <brownf@bigbrain.com> 2009, 'Using the Web more efficiently', discussion group, National Computer Network, viewed 23 April 2009, <observe@abc.net.com>.

Needling, T 2009, *Trevor's Holiday in Tasmania*, Weblog, Viewed 19 March 2009, http://needling.info.

Barnes, S 2009, 'What happened to our great Sportsmen?', *Beijing Blog*, Weblog post 25 February 2009, http://blogs.abc.net.au/olympics/.

Quantitative Methods 2008, 'Focus Groups', Wiki article, 3 January, viewed 5 February 2009, <http://wiki.iosa.it/dockuwiki/focusgroups>.

Seedogrun 2008, *Inside the making of Memory the movie*, online video, viewed 4 February 2009, <http://youtube.com/watch?v=EXg3w_j6Kec>.

Are blogs the new newspapers?, podcast, PodcastAlley, 19 March, accessed 20 March 2009, <http://www.podcastalley.com/forum/showthread.php?t=146809>.

2.9.7 Personal email message

Normally, email messages are not included in the LOR and they are treated the same way as personal communications (see section 2.6.10). Where it is necessary, however, the general format for citing a personal email message is as follows:

<Sender's name with initial preceding surname>, <email>, <Date of email>, <email address>.

A Elsworth, email, 10 August 2009,<elswortha@ugt.edu.au>.

Note: It is critical that you obtain the sender's permission before publishing their email address.

2.10 Films, videos, television and on-line images

The title, date of recording, format, publisher, place of recording and any special credits should be listed (*Style manual* 2002, p. 229) as shown in the following examples.

Film:

Learning to live 2008, motion picture, London, Fine Films Inc., producer Martin Freeth.

Video recording or television:

What are we going to do with the money?, video recording, ABC Television, Sydney, 8 August 2008.

On-line image:

If there is no author, put the image title first followed by the date, otherwise use the person or organisation responsible for the image.

Australia 2007, Country Map, Mapquest, United Kingdom, viewed 5 March 2009, <http://www.mapquest.co.uk/mp/maps/mapAddress.do>.

Rafter, R 2004, *Lunar Eclipse*, viewed 3 March 2009, <http://images.google.com.au/imgres?imgurl=http://www.raftermranch.com/RafterMRanch/Lunar>.

2.11 Summary

To prepare a well-balanced written assignment, wide reading and research are required. Interpretation of the thoughts, ideas and research findings of other writers is essential. This process allows the development of a personal perspective on the topic and gives the written work credibility and depth. Referencing serves the professional purpose of allowing subsequent researchers to reanalyse and reinterpret the written work if they choose to work on the topic or issue.

However, material included from other sources must be correctly referenced or the author may be accused of plagiarism. Correct referencing is not only an ethical requirement of any written work, it is a legal one.

The important points to note from this chapter are:

1 Plagiarism and collusion are unacceptable.
2 Students must:

■ reference other authors' material used in written assignment work by providing both in-text references and an LOR

■ use the methods described in this handbook when formatting in-text references and lists of references.

2.12 Example of the Harvard referencing system

The following is an example of how to use the Harvard system:

You'd hear them passing in the street, front doors closing, soft voices, muffled footsteps. Then the first mill whistles at seven o'clock, telling you it was time to get up. Those whistles regulated your life, whether or not you worked in the mills. I never got used to it when they stopped (Glenda Jansen 2008, pers. comm., 23 June).

The textile mills of Geelong were mostly silent during the early 1970s, when the full effects of the downturn in the textile industry were felt. Geelong 's textile workforce was virtually halved, and sackings ran at 60 per day over 1975 (Anderson 1977; *Geelong Advertiser* 1974). The Textile Workers Union had 3364 members in the Geelong district in 1971; two years later this number had dropped to 1398 (Hughes 1977, p. 10).

The decline led inevitably to widespread mill closures. Another notable consequence was a shift in the division of labour: men, who constituted only 42 per cent of the workforce in the mills operating in 1961 (Australian Textile Workers Union 1961), comprised a 61 per cent majority in 1986 (Australian Bureau of Statistics 1986).

The painful restructuring during these years had a traumatic impact on both male- and female-dominated areas of employment. While women in the textile, clothing and footwear industries were laid off in increasing numbers, men in the car and aluminium industries were equally hard hit during the global rationalisation that followed the oil crises of the 1970s (Hughes 1977; Linge & McKay 1981; Rich 1987).

List of References

Anderson, H 1977, 'The mill workers of the 1970s', *Network World*, vol. 14, no. 4, p. 4, viewed 10 March 2002, ABI/INFORM database, item: 01363555.

Australian Bureau of Statistics 1986, *Census of population and housing. Local government area, Geelong statistical district*, Australian Government Publishing Service, Canberra.

Australian Textile Workers Union 1961, weekly employment records in Geelong by mill, unpublished report.

Geelong Advertiser 1974, 'All in a day's work', Monday 24 July, p. 30.

Hughes, W 1977, 'The state of the textile industry', *Textile Topics*, vol. 1, no. 16, pp. 10–12.

Linge, G & McKay, J 1981, *Structural change in Australia: some spatial and organisational responses*, HG/15 Research School of Pacific Studies, Canberra.

Rich, D 1987, *The industrial geography of Australia*, Methuen, North Ryde, NSW.

(Adapted from Deakin University 1993, *Faculty of Arts style guide*, Geelong, pp. 10–11.)

2.13 List of References

The following references were used to prepare this chapter. Readers who want more information on referencing may also find these useful.

Commonwealth of Australia 2002, *Style manual for authors, editors and printers*, 6th edn, John Wiley & Sons, Brisbane.

Electronic sources: APA style of citation n.d., viewed 6 May 1997, <www.uvm. edu/~ncrane/estyles/apa.html>.

Electronic sources: MLA style of citation n.d., viewed 6 May 1997, <www.uvm. edu/~ncrane/estyles/mla.html>.

Guides to citing electronic information n.d., viewed 6 May 1997, <http:// mahogany.lib.utexas.edu/Libs/PCL/Cite.html>.

ISO 1997, *Excerpts from final draft International Standard ISO 690-2*, viewed 9 May 1997, <www.nlc-bnc.ca/iso/tc46sc9/standard/690-2e.htm>.

Lamp, J n.d., *Citation styles for electronic media*, viewed 9 May 1997, <http:// lamp.cs.utas.edu.au/citation.html>.

Lee, MT 1996, *Guidelines for citing references and electronic sources of information*, viewed 6 May 1997, <www.eliz.tased.edu.au/refs.htm>.

Li, X & Crane, NB 1993, *Electronic style: a guide to citing electronic information*, Mecklermedia, Westport, CT.

Page, ME 1996, *A brief citation guide for Internet sources in history and the humanities*, viewed 9 May 1997, ver.2.1, <http://h-net2.msu.edu/~africa/citation.html>.

Referencing Internet resources using the Harvard system n.d., viewed 8 May 1997, <www.usq.edu.au/library/pubsexms/elecinfo/citing1.htm>.

Walker, JR 1996, *MLA-style citations of electronic sources*, viewed 6 May 1997, <www.cas.usf.edu/english/walker/mla.html>.

Note: the following (revised) edition of Li and Crane (1993) is now available:

Li, X & Crane, NB 1996, *Electronic style: a guide to citing electronic information*, Information Today, Medford, NJ.

3 | Report writing[1]

3.1 Introduction

All written assignments must follow specific structures that allow the document to be easily read and understood. This chapter provides a useful guide for students preparing written work in a formal report format. A formal report should contain the following sections, in the order given:

1 Assignment cover sheet
2 Letter of transmittal (not always required — check your instructions)
3 Title page
4 Executive summary
5 Table of contents
6 Introduction
7 The body
8 Conclusions
9 Recommendations (sometimes not required)
10 List of references (LOR)
11 Glossary (not always required)
12 Appendices

3.2 Report structure

This section provides detailed guidance on each section of the formal report listed.

3.2.1 Assignment cover sheet

The cover sheet protects the assignment and identifies the student and the due date. It also provides verification of submission date and authentication of original work through the student's signature. This signature on the statement of original work is legally binding and means that the student agrees that any unoriginal work in the assignment has been appropriately referenced. Some universities provide assignment and course specific cover sheets for students to use.

3.2.2 Letter of transmittal

A letter of transmittal enables the writer of the report to establish contact with the receiver, and acts as the formal record of delivery of the report.

The letter of transmittal should be fully left-justified (with the exception of the sender's address) and should use open punctuation (no commas or full stops in the address or heading section of the letter). In general, letters of transmittal use single spacing within the parts of the letter and double spacing between the parts (i.e. paragraphs or heading and greeting). See figure 3.1 for an example.

---

1 The contribution to this section by Cec Pederson is gratefully acknowledged.

Mr Warren Vale
NewIdeas Pty Ltd
54 Phillip Street
TOWNSVILLE QLD 4810

Dear Mr Vale

Further to your request of 23 July, I hereby attach our report analysing the market potential for the new product you are assessing. As discussed with you during our meeting last month, we have paid particular attention in our analysis to the consumer decision-making processes of your target market.

The report provides a detailed breakdown of the product's possible impact in the marketplace, as well as a full examination of your direct and indirect competitors.

Our investigations suggest that this product has good market potential in the current economic conditions. However, as outlined in our report, indications of possible competition from South-East Asian producers within the next decade suggest the need for an accelerated development program in order to establish a niche in the new market. We recommend that your company proceed with the development of the product, with consideration given to the revised schedule provided in this report.

We have proposed a number of ways in which you might counter potential foreign competition while maximising your domestic sales profile. None of these proposals, we believe, need affect product development but several suggestions hold the promise of broadening the potential domestic market in surprising directions. We discuss these points in detail in the report.

Thank you for affording us the opportunity to work with you on this project. I will be glad to discuss any questions you may have at our meeting next week.

Yours sincerely

M. Ehrlich

Martin Ehrlich — Director

FIGURE 3.1 Example of a letter of transmittal

The letter should be addressed to the person who requested the report (in your assignments it is permissible to use a fictitious person), and the return address of the sender should be left-justified, unless official letterhead is used (your name should not appear at this point). The city and state elements of the sender's return address and of the receiver's address should be entered in capital letters.

The date of writing should be in the format *day/month/year*, with the month written in full and not abbreviated as a number (e.g. *3 March 2009* and not *3/3/09*). Avoid the use of suffixes such as *st* or *th* after the day (i.e. do not write *4th March*).

The body of the letter of transmittal should generally take the form of a 'good or neutral news' letter (although in some cases a 'bad news' letter may be appropriate). That is, it should contain:

- *a positive opening:* usually a straightforward statement indicating that the report is enclosed

- *further explanation:* generally includes a brief overview of the report, as well as brief details of the conclusions reached. Acknowledgement of any people who assisted in the report's preparation may be included here

- *a goodwill message:* a courteous closing in which you indicate what has to be done next, express your pleasure at being able to provide the information in the report and state your willingness to discuss the report in person. Refer to the example in figure 3.1.

3.2.3 Title page

The title page is placed after the cover sheet and letter of transmittal and should provide the following:

- the title of the report, or restatement of assignment or essay question, usually also indicating the question number if a choice is given

- the name of the person for whom the report was prepared (instructor or client); sometimes the tutorial group or tutor's name is also required

- the date of submission of the report

- the student's name and student number.

Some instructors also require a statement of the length of the report (number of words). If required this should also appear on the title page.

Note: a title page is essential for all assessment items regardless of how they are submitted. This means that electronically submitted assessment items should also have a title page with the same information. See figure 3.2 for an example of a title page.

3.2.4 Executive summary

The executive summary provides the reader with the report's major purpose, the analytical processes, the findings and the recommendations. It is so called because executives traditionally do not have sufficient time to read complete reports, yet need to extract sufficient information to make informed decisions. The executive summary should encourage the reader to go on to read the full report. It can also serve as a quick reference for the writer of the report at some future stage.

```
┌─────────────────────────────────────────────────┐
│         A REPORT ON THE OPERATIONS OF           │
│        AUSTRALIAN McDONALD'S STORES, 2009       │
│                                                 │
│            Prepared for: Dr AJ BLOGGS           │
│                                                 │
│             Submitted: 10 March 2009            │
│                                                 │
│                                   Prepared by:  │
│                         AJ STUDENT 001005009    │
│                         BF GRADUATE 001004008   │
│                         RU CURIOUS 001006007    │
│                                                 │
└─────────────────────────────────────────────────┘
```

FIGURE 3.2 Example of an assignment title page

The executive summary is an extremely important component of any formal report and should be prepared *carefully*, rather than as an afterthought. Several drafts will be necessary to get it 'right'.

The executive summary will rarely be more than one page in length and should not contain subheadings, direct quotes, bullet points or unnecessary descriptive information. It should also be single-line spaced. It should contain a brief statement of the following:

- the purpose (objectives) and scope of the report
- the type of analysis conducted (and methods used)
- the most important and significant findings, in summary form
- the most important and significant recommendations.

It should be a 'stand-alone' document that encompasses the important points of the report it accompanies. Table 3.1 provides a guide to the approximate length of the executive summary.

TABLE 3.1 A guide to the length of an executive summary	
REPORT LENGTH (WORDS)	**EXECUTIVE SUMMARY LENGTH (WORDS)**
1500	200–300
2000	250–350
3000	450–550

Note: The word count of the report does not include the executive summary, letter of transmittal, table of contents, figures, tables, references or appendices.

Most people recommend that the executive summary be written last, after the report has been prepared. This does not mean that it appears last in the report. It simply recognises that once the report is completed and the conclusions and recommendations have been made, it is far easier to write an overall summary of that report. Avoid providing executive summaries that read like a table of contents. That is, do not just list the things you did in the order you did them; it should really be more of a summary of the main activities and findings of the report.

The executive summary should be given a page number using the lower-case roman numeral *i* (if it runs to a second page, this should be marked with a *ii*). Remember also that the executive summary must appear before the table of contents.

3.2.5 Table of contents

The table of contents should be listed on a new page of the report and, as for the executive summary, this page is numbered using a roman numeral (e.g. *ii*). Sections are listed in the order in which they appear in the report and the corresponding page numbers should be shown. Page 1 of the report, usually the introduction, follows the table of contents, and all subsequent sections are then numbered sequentially using Arabic numerals (*2, 3, 4* etc.).

When setting out your table of contents, the main section numbers should appear against the left-hand margin. There should then be one tab space to the heading of that section. Corresponding subsection numbers should appear indented one tab space from the left-hand margin, or under the first letter of the main heading, and subsection headings indented a further tab space to the right. Dot leaders may be used between the entry and page number to improve the clarity of the document. There are generally single spaces between subsections and double spaces between sections (see figure 3.3).

If a section covers more than one page, only the page number on which the section begins need be shown in the table of contents.

Note: If submitting a report with a computer-generated table of contents, the formatting guideline outlined here might not strictly apply. Compare the table of contents at the front of this handbook, generated by computer, with the manually constructed one shown in figure 3.3. Care should be taken to follow the example shown in figure 3.3 as closely as possible.

Sub-subsections should be treated in a similar fashion; that is, two tab spaces from the left-hand margin or under the first letter of the subheading title. Again, refer to the example provided in figure 3.3. It is essential that all major headings and subheadings be clearly identifiable.

All appendices should be listed with their titles and corresponding page numbers. Following this, tables, then figures and then graphs should also be listed separately with their titles and corresponding page numbers. See section 1.3.3 for differences between tables and figures.

3.2.6 Introduction

The introduction has three parts:

- *the authorisation and purpose of the report:* tell the reader who has commissioned the work and why the report is being produced

TABLE OF CONTENTS   **Page**

ii

FIGURE 3.3   Sample table of contents

- *hindrances:* any limitations encountered in the production of the report that may affect the results or the ability of the writer to complete the report

- *the scope of the report:* summarise what the report covers, how information will be presented in the report, where the information for the report comes from and how it will be gathered (e.g. questionnaires or other research). Be careful here once again not to simply reproduce the table of contents: this should be an overview or summary of what will be done, not a bit-by-bit reproduction. Focus on the important elements.

3.2.7   Body

This is the main part of the report and contains the discussions and analysis. The information in this section should be presented in a logical sequence, using paragraphing to separate ideas. As a general rule, each paragraph should contain one main idea. Headings and subheadings should be used to identify each section and introduce new ideas or directions.

It is *very important* in this section to ensure that theoretical evidence or research findings are used to support the discussion. Throughout the report, answers should be provided to the following questions:

- How is this known? (Usually some sort of reference is needed to address this question.)

- Why is this so? (Here you would cite research findings or results from investigations of data and information. You may also use theoretical frameworks to support your findings.)

- Why was this option selected? (You need to justify your approach and recommendations using theory and research results.)

- Why was this course of action or design selected? (Here you may consider implementation issues and reiterate research findings and theoretical support.)

3.2.8   Conclusions

This section should essentially summarise the main points or findings of the assignment. It should be based on the information presented in the body. It is essential that you do not introduce any new information or ideas at this stage and the use of direct quotations should be avoided. The conclusion should answer the question: what do the findings mean?

It is important to ensure that your conclusions are consistent with the outline given in the introduction. For this reason, it is generally recommended that the introduction be written after the main report. The conclusion should answer the following questions. Was the purpose of the report fulfilled? Have the specified sources of information been used? Have the areas stated been adequately tackled?

3.2.9   Recommendations

Recommendations should be presented only when asked for. They are based on the conclusions and are the suggested options for solving the problem or problems that made writing the report necessary. Recommendations should be brief statements outlining a specific course of action suggested by your research, for example, 'That library hours be extended to 11.00 pm on weeknights'.

It should be clearly demonstrated that detailed thought has been given to how the recommendations should be *implemented*, as well as what the resource *implications* might be for these. Consider the following questions:

- Are the recommendations *realistic* in the light of current environmental conditions (economic times, likely competitor reaction, government policy and consumer reactions)?

- Has sufficient thought been given to *timing* and *priorities*? When do the recommendations need to be implemented and in what order?

- Are the proposals *feasible*? Are there the financial, physical and human resources to support them?

3.2.10 Bibliography or LOR

Remember, an *LOR* is an alphabetical listing of any material actually *cited* in the report. A *bibliography* is an alphabetical listing of all the sources of information that have been read, used or referenced in researching and preparing the report. A bibliography will, therefore, contain any additional information that was reviewed in compiling the report, whether or not it was specifically cited. While a formal report may require the inclusion of both, generally *only an LOR is required in student assignments*.

3.2.11 Glossary

A glossary is required only if a considerable number of technical terms have been used in the report, which may need to be explained to the reader. It is a form of minidictionary. It should start on a separate page. The term to be explained should be entered on the left and a definition, or reference, added on the right.

Be sure to reference correctly any definitions that have been taken from another author's work.

3.2.12 Appendices

Appendices generally contain:

- material that is too bulky to include in the body of the report
- material that is essential to explain a point but that if included in the body of the report, would distract the reader from the main message.

All appendices should be numbered sequentially (i.e. *1, 2, 3* and so on) and given a title. It is essential that direct reference be made in the main body of the report to each appendix. This will enable the reader to understand the material presented in the appendix in the context of the report.

Each appendix should begin on a new page, and each should usually contain only one major piece of information. However, if you have a number of tables, figures or graphs in which the information is interrelated, then an appendix can contain more than one piece of information. There is no limit to the number of appendices you can have (providing they are relevant).

Appendices usually include questionnaires, charts, maps, tables, extracts and so on. *It is very important that any material included in appendices is referenced correctly*. For example, if using a diagram from a textbook, there must be a reference for the source of that diagram.

3.3 Summary

A report is a special type of written communication used to provide concise information, and in some cases opinions, on a specific subject. Reports should be structured so that readers are guided through the main points. All relevant information should be included so that, after reading the report, readers will have a clear understanding of the key issues concerned.

Although most reports follow a fairly standard format, report layout may vary depending on the intended audience. Formal reports should include an assignment cover sheet, title page, letter of transmittal, executive summary, table of contents, introduction, the main body of the report, conclusions, recommendations, LOR, glossary (if required) and appendices. Each of these components has been discussed in detail in this chapter.

4 | The case study[1]

4.1 Introduction

A case study is a written description of a business problem or situation at a specific moment in time — it may be described as 'a snapshot in time'. A case study analysis is the critical review of that case information in combination with other secondary data to identify the problems or issues that are (or should be) important to that organisation. A formal case report is the written presentation of the analysis conducted, demonstrating your understanding of the problems from both a theoretical and a practical perspective. The case report recommends solutions for those problems based on a theoretical framework. Some courses may ask for a less formal style of case report; however, the appropriate methods of analysis remain the same. You need to check your assignment instructions to establish the style of report required for your particular assessment task.

Sometimes, the organisation on which the case was based will be disguised. Usually, however, the actual organisation name and names of the people in that organisation are used. Cases include important information that has a bearing on the issues central to the case analysis. However, it is also common for cases to have seemingly irrelevant pieces of information (called 'red herrings') which give a more rounded picture of the organisation and the general environment at the time of writing. It is important to differentiate between what is important and what is just background information.

You will encounter much variation from course to course on what is called a 'case study'. The **Harvard MBA** case study format is used mainly in advanced subjects and postgraduate courses and usually demands a detailed and lengthy discussion about an organisation. This style of case study requires students to analyse the problem or problems and ultimately provide decision recommendations and implementation plans.

Another type of case study that students will encounter is a **short case** (one to three pages). These type of cases provide a less formal description of an organisation or business situation. Questions that require students to apply theoretical arguments or analytical skills (or both) in their answers are often attached to this form of case study. Some lecturers may also use the term 'case study' when they require students to give practical examples or to describe scenarios.

Whichever form you encounter, case studies are designed to provide students with opportunities to experience the challenges faced in real-life situations and to use a knowledge of a particular theoretical framework to provide solutions to these challenges.

---

1 The contribution to this section by Cec Pederson is gratefully acknowledged.

The main objectives of any case study are:

- to help students learn to apply various theories through simulated problem solving and decision making
- to allow students to learn by doing through the application of principles, rather than through passive learning forms such as listening to lecturers and reading textbooks
- to allow students to reinforce and apply theories and concepts in managerial contexts.

The information contained in this chapter is based on the longer Harvard case study format but it can be applied generally to each of the case study formats mentioned.

Given the variety of ways in which case studies are used, you may be given specific instructions by your instructor about how to structure your case report. These directions may differ in detail from the information contained in this chapter. Check your assignment instructions for this. However, if no specific information is provided, use the format presented here.

A final note with case analysis. Cases often have issues that can be considered from a number of different management perspectives. It is important to consider the context of the course you are studying to help you interpret the appropriate case issues. For example, a case may be set for a marketing course and may also have considerable human resource issues and maybe even finance issues embedded in it. If you are studying **marketing** though, you should focus on the '**marketing**' aspects of the case and consider how (if at all) these other management issues affect the **marketing** elements of the case. If you are studying a management course, then maybe you will need to consider these other issues.

4.2 Preparing a case analysis

The case analysis technique requires a great deal of creativity but this gets easier with practice (Kashani 1993). It is important to recognise that there is no one correct solution to a case study. There may be a number of feasible strategies that management could adopt, each having different implications for the future of the company and involving different trade-offs. A good case analysis will allow students, drawing on the data gathered and on the relevant theory, to put forward a report that has recommendations based on strong, well-presented and supported arguments (Lovelock 1992).

Just as there is no single correct answer in case analysis, there is also no one 'best way' to complete the analysis. However, a number of generally recommended procedures will help students to achieve a satisfactory result. Often, the major problem for students when faced with a case study is 'Where do I begin?'. The following advice should help to overcome that problem:

- *Read* the case through once *without* taking any notes or highlighting points of interest or importance.

- *Leave* the case for at least 24 hours. During that time, review your textbooks or study notes for the theoretical implications of the material contained in the case. You are looking for general theoretical themes here that may help you to identify the problems or issues more clearly in the next stages of the analysis process. It will also help to keep you focused on the relevant theoretical framework and to identify other instances where these issues may have arisen in different organisations.

- *Reread* the case, this time making notes and highlighting areas that seem important or inconsistent with the general direction of the material. At this stage you are really only 'fishing': looking for anything that stands out. This is often a good time to manipulate the data in any financial tables — to calculate ratios, percentage increases and decreases and differences between years, for example. This will often form the basis for your future analysis. Do not attempt to formulate too many answers at this point. You are looking only for trends, inconsistencies and a general overview of the company and the situation. You should be asking yourself lots of questions at this stage.

- *Organise* the information you have noted. See if you can group the information into logical categories (i.e. these are all product development issues or these are all industrial relations issues) and from these groupings look for potential answers to the questions you are posing for the company and the possible reasons for those problems that you have noted. Identify any areas about which you need more information, perhaps using other sources such as textbooks, journals, newspapers and the business press. You might ask yourself the following questions:

  - What sort of organisation does the case concern?

  - What is the nature of the industry (broadly defined)?

  - What is going on in the external environment?

  - What issues do management seem to be facing?

  - How can any tables or figures provided be used to further the analysis?

  - Can new insights be gained by combining or recalculating data presented in the case (e.g. using ratios or percentages or comparing years)?

  - What is really happening in this situation? Quite often you will need to 'read between the lines' in order to better understand the issues. Do not take as fact the perspective, hints and biases the case writer or the management of the company is giving (Kashani 1993).

- One way to help you make sense at this stage of the information you are compiling is to use strategic analysis tools such as a *situation analysis* or a *SWOT analysis* (there are many others you might also use, these are just two of the more common ones). These tools will provide a framework within which you can organise and clarify relevant information and the relationships that may exist between issues. Section 4.4 discusses both of these techniques in detail. Some courses will require these tools to be used; others will not. Indeed, such tools may be totally inappropriate for some case studies, especially the shorter versions with questions attached. It is a good idea to check your assignment instructions for more information about what is required in this area.

- Begin to gather more general information about the company, or about the industry within which this organisation operates. This background information will help you to better understand the context of the problems and possible industry trends. You may also need to be aware of the external environment at the time of the case; for example, what was the economy doing, and what were the social norms?

- Begin drafting your report using the headings and components discussed in the next section (see also chapters 1 and 2 for more information on the writing style and referencing format required). Before you start this stage, ensure you have spent sufficient time on the analysis. Do not be tempted to arrive at a quick solution. It is also very important not to identify with the organisation in the case. You should adopt a third-person view about what you believe it should or should not do. So avoid sentences that begin, *We should*. Remember, too, that you should beware of being misled by management's own views of what the issues are.

- *Discuss* your results when you reach the first draft stage. Get together with a small group of your fellow students (preferably those who you know are at a similar stage in the project) and discuss your findings and, most important, your recommendations and reasoning. This allows you to check that you have thought things through and have not overlooked any vital information. It is important that you do not use this session to 'check' your answers. Rather, it is an opportunity to revise your arguments in the light of different perspectives. Do not worry if your answers differ from those of your friends. You may have used different reference material or approached the problem differently. Remember though that it is generally a requirement that you submit individual work so beware of aligning your answers too closely with those of your colleagues. This could be seen as collusion which will be treated as academic misconduct.

- *Polish* your report, proofread for spelling, typos and grammatical errors. Double-check all referencing and ensure that all appendices are attached.

4.3 The structure of the case analysis report

When presenting your results, the case report format varies slightly from a traditional report format (see section 3.1). Generally, in a case study you are given detailed information about an organisation or situation, and you are required to analyse this information, to identify the problems correctly, to demonstrate an understanding of the causes and effects of the problems and to provide recommended solutions based on a theoretical framework.

A formal case report generally has the following sections:

1 Assignment cover page
2 Letter of transmittal (not always required)
3 Title page
4 Executive summary
5 Table of contents
6 Introduction or case background
7 Body of the analysis, which includes the following subheadings:
   (i) Problem identification or identification of case issues
   (ii) Problem analysis and justification
8 Alternative solutions
9 Recommendations
10 Implementation plan (if requested)
11 List of references
12 Appendices

You will note that this format differs somewhat from the report style discussed in chapter 3. Because points 1 to 5 are discussed thoroughly in that chapter, they will not be reviewed here. Rather, points 6 to 11 (which either are not discussed or have requirements that differ from those covered in chapter 3) are discussed in more detail with the aid of the following example (McArthur 1997).

A sample case scenario

Marilyn White was a meticulous and detail-minded employee who was promoted to a supervisory position almost a year ago. Over the past few months there have been problems within Marilyn's department. Marilyn allows no initiative on the part of her employees. She insists on checking every piece of work that leaves the department, with the result that her subordinates spend large amounts of time waiting for her to check their work, or redoing work that does not meet her exacting standards. Consequently, productivity is low. Staff morale is poor, a number of members having left the organisation or being on the point of leaving. Marilyn herself is increasingly stressed. What can be done about Marilyn?

4.3.1 Introduction or case background

This section should provide a short summary of the current background of the case and should lead to the issues confronting management. This section should be no longer than one-third to one-half of a page. It should 'set the scene' for your analysis.

One way to begin organising your thoughts for this part of the process is to list what you see as the main points in the case. For example, the main ideas from the scenario above are shown in figure 4.1 overleaf. You will need to summarise these points to write your introduction. (Do not use bullet points in your case report, although they are a good idea in your rough drafts).

- Marilyn was recently promoted to supervisor based upon attributes of meticulousness and attention to detail.

- Marilyn's supervisory behaviour can be characterised as:
  - allowing no initiative from employees
  - insisting on checking all work against her exacting standards
  - ordering work not up to her standards to be redone.

- Employees have idle time because they have to wait for Marilyn to check their work.

- Employees have to spend double the time on a job they have to redo to meet Marilyn's standards.

- Productivity is low.

- Staff morale is low, partly because of loss, and pending loss, of staff from her department.

- Marilyn is increasingly stressed.

FIGURE 4.1 An example of a list of main points

4.3.2 Body of the analysis

In this section you are required to list briefly the main issues or problems in the case and then to discuss why they are problems with reference to the appropriate theory and examples. The two parts to this section are:

- *problem identification*, sometimes referred to as *identification of case issues* (check your assignment instructions for required terminology)

- *problem analysis and justification*.

1. Problem identification or identification of case issues

Some issues you identify may not be problems as such. Rather, a number of issues may need to be resolved before they become problems or perhaps there are opportunities that have not been identified effectively or exploited. Whether they are issues or problems, it is important that they be identified clearly and precisely and, when there is more than one, that they be prioritised.

It is also important to define the case problems or issues in terms of the specific concepts or relevant theories you are studying. If the course is on consumer behaviour, use consumer behaviour terminology or theory, not general marketing theory, in your statement of issues. Similarly, if it is an industrial relations course, apply that theory and not general human resources theory. Your instructor will want you to focus on the issues relevant to the particular subject. This approach will also allow you to communicate better and to focus on solutions relevant to the issues you have identified.

A case study is often built around several interrelated problems or issues. In order to make sense of these, and to organise them usefully, you need to adopt a systematic and logical approach that will enable you to get to the heart of the problem. Often, the problem or issue may not be evident and you will have to sift through the information, teasing out particulars that are *symptoms* related to the problem itself. As you identify the symptoms, you will be building up evidence that will point to the major cause or underlying *problem*. Remember to look closely at the information in the introduction. It is most important at this stage that you do not stray from the actual evidence contained in the case.

Of each symptom, ask the question *What caused this?* and note your answers. You may find that you can then ask the question again, and this time the chances are high that you will reach the source of the problem or issue. When you have finished listing the symptoms and no longer have anything of which you can ask *What caused this?*, you should be able to identify the problem or issue. Table 4.1 presents an example of this process applied to the example scenario. In this case, the problem is evident: it is Marilyn's supervisory style. You can see in this example that if you were to list all the items categorised here as symptoms, you would not really be getting to the heart of the problem, and you would not achieve maximum marks.

TABLE 4.1	Example of problem identification process	
ISSUES IDENTIFIED FROM THE CASE	**GROUPING OF ISSUES ACCORDING TO THEORY**	**AND WHAT CAUSED THIS?**
■ Marilyn insists on checking all work. ■ Marilyn insists on staff redoing work not up to her exacting standards.	Low productivity	Marilyn's supervisory style
■ Staff spend idle time waiting for Marilyn. ■ Staff have to redo work, doubling the time necessary to produce the product. ■ Staff initiative is not permitted.	Low staff morale	Marilyn's supervisory style
■ Staff initiative is not permitted. ■ Staff spend too much time idle, waiting for Marilyn to check finished work.	Staff turnover increasing	Marilyn's supervisory style

In this situation you would state that the main problem is Marilyn's supervisory style, as evidenced by the low productivity of her staff, their low morale and the high staff turnover.

2. Problem analysis and justification

Now that you have identified the problem, this section answers the question: why is this a problem? To answer this, you need to:

■ identify the underlying causes of the problems (How has Marilyn's supervisory style reached this level or been allowed to develop this way?)

- justify why they are problems by using supporting concepts, theoretical frameworks and other material from your course of study (column 2 in table 4.1)

- examine the effects of the problems on the organisation (column 1 in table 4.1).

Here you can start to hypothesise (to guess in an informed way using logic and problem-solving techniques such as brainstorming) the factors that have brought about these problems or issues. This is where you should consider the relevant theories and theoretical issues that relate to the situation. You will need to have theoretical support and demonstrate evidence of wide reading by including referenced content from other authors. Remember, you will considerably improve both your analysis and your final grade if you can demonstrate an understanding of the theoretical concepts from the relevant course of study by applying these to the case.

You will also need to demonstrate, through your discussion, that you have an understanding of the organisation, the industry and the external environment.

You should use this section to explore the options available to the organisation, and to identify and develop the theoretical implications of these options. Figure 4.2 gives an example of the issues that might be explored from the sample scenario. Answers to each of the questions posed at this stage will also lead in the direction of *possible* solutions.

In the scenario given, you might well raise the following questions:

- Which of the company's selection procedures has resulted in the selection of a person on criteria other than those that might be expected to be important in a supervisor (e.g. leadership style)? Are there any theories that would support or explain this?

- Why has there not been an improvement in the quality of output by the workforce as the 'new' standards are recognised? What are the relationships between Marilyn and the rest of her workers? Why are they not responding positively? What does the theory say about this? Is it a common occurrence? Why? What solutions does the theory propose for this?

- Has Marilyn been given supervisory training? What kinds of training does the theory say she should have had, when and why?

- Has Marilyn been mentored in her job? What does the theory on mentoring say about this?

- What is the culture of the organisation? What does the theory say about the role of organisational culture in supervision and is it relevant or helpful in explaining what has happened here?

- What was Marilyn's predecessor's style? What does the theory say about this as a factor and how is it important in this analysis and the search for solutions?

FIGURE 4.2 Example of problem analysis process

4.3.3 Formulation of alternatives or possible solutions

Before recommending a course of action, you must examine alternative ways that the problem or issue can be solved or resolved. It is important that a range of alternative courses of action is fully evaluated before one or more are ultimately selected (Kashani 1993). Remember that there is more than one solution to most management issues.

This section, then, answers the question *What are the options?* It should also explain in some detail why the proposed alternatives are appropriate. The question to be asked of each alternative is, *If this is done, or not done, then what?* It is important to remember that the alternatives you suggest should be consistent with the environment in which the firm is operating, be persuasive in their promise to solve the problem and, ultimately, be implementable. You may also need to think of alternatives in terms of short-term tactics and long-term strategies.

A good starting point is to list the alternatives in point form. Alternatives may not be mutually exclusive. A combination of actions may be appropriate. Each alternative should be explored in terms of its feasibility and the potential consequences of its adoption. In the case of the sample scenario, the list of possible alternatives might resemble that in figure 4.3.

1.	Do nothing.
2.	Fire/sack/dismiss Marilyn.
3.	Transfer Marilyn.
4.	Counsel Marilyn for stress and leadership style.
5.	Train Marilyn.
6.	Mentor Marilyn.
7.	Give team training to the whole department.
8.	Check management policy regarding selection, supervisor manual and mentoring.
9.	Train management in quality service techniques, teamwork and empowerment.

FIGURE 4.3 List of alternative actions

When making *What if?* judgements, or decisions about the advantages and disadvantages of alternative actions and combinations of actions, you should use the main issues or problems that have been identified in the first section as a framework for evaluation. Remember that, ultimately, the proposed solutions need to resolve the issues or problems you have identified, so their relative merits should be considered in those terms. In many case studies there is a need to solve immediate issues or problems and then to advise medium- to longer-term strategies. In our scenario, time is very much a factor. Something should be done *now*. This should not, however, limit adoption of a wider view. See table 4.2 for examples of analysis of the alternatives for the sample scenario. Take each of the possible solutions and evaluate it in point form to build up a framework for the discussion in your report.

Three last points on the formulation and evaluation of alternatives.

1 When preparing action alternatives, do not discard any option without first evaluating it at some length.
2 Before finalising your suggestions, try to think through the mechanics of how they are supposed to work. Ask yourself, 'What are the critical steps and how will they help solve the main issues or problems identified?'.
3 Once you have chosen which option or combination of options to adopt, think about possible criticisms the plan might encounter. This advance mental preparation will help you to develop a more persuasive argument to support the course of action you have chosen.

TABLE 4.2	Evaluating alternative actions	
	POSSIBLE SOLUTION	**THEN WHAT?**
1.	Do nothing.	▪ Problem persists (and might get worse). ▪ Increased loss of productivity and increased costs.
2.	Fire/sack/dismiss Marilyn.	▪ Loss of an asset. ▪ Replacement cost. ▪ Unless new criteria for selection are used, another Marilyn might emerge.
3.	Transfer Marilyn.	▪ Loss of an asset. ▪ Could still cause same problem in a new place. ▪ Still have to find a suitable replacement.
4.	Counsel Marilyn for stress and leadership style.	▪ Should work, okay for immediate solution, but must be complemented by other actions.
5.	Train Marilyn.	▪ Weigh up cost vs benefit. ▪ Could increase her asset worth.
6.	Mentor Marilyn.	▪ Weigh up cost vs benefit. ▪ Need to find a suitable person. ▪ Gains to be made in the long term.
7.	Introduce team training.	▪ Potential for great benefit. ▪ Cost and loss of some productivity in short term but gains to be made in long term.
8.	Review management policies.	▪ Assistance needed (consultant). ▪ Cost. ▪ Benefits in medium and long term.
9.	Train management in quality processes.	▪ Will have the ability to model new practice. ▪ Potential benefits from empowerment.

4.3.4 Recommendations or choice of solutions

This section of your report will answer the question *What should be done?* It should be based on the previous section's analysis and should be relatively brief, since the discussion of the advantages of the proposed solutions was covered in the previous section, where the alternatives were evaluated. Depending on the type of case and the number of issues or problems identified, several recommendations may be made in this section. Recommendations should be prioritised and there should be a very brief reiteration of the main reasons these options should be chosen. You may wish to subdivide this section into short-term and long-term solutions. See figure 4.4 for examples of recommendations that might be applied to the sample scenario.

From consideration of the options proposed in table 4.2, it is suggested that the firm adopt options 4, 5, 6, 7, 8 and 9.

The most important course of action — which should be implemented immediately — is to counsel Marilyn about her leadership style and to give her appropriate mentoring. As soon as possible after this, she should also be given some directed supervisory training. In recognition of the difficulties under which Marilyn's team has been working, it is also important that the work group receive assistance. Some form of intervention is necessary and it is suggested that the use of a consultant to study group dynamics with them could help overcome their problems and get them working well together.

In the short- and medium-terms, the advantages of management adopting and being trained in quality service processes should be given serious consideration. The benefits that would accrue from such a strategy would help minimise the chances of this situation recurring.

FIGURE 4.4   Recommendations

4.3.5 Implementation plan

Your recommendations will not be complete unless you give some thought to how your proposed strategy should be implemented. So the details of implementation must be presented. The implementation plan should also provide persuasive evidence for gaining acceptance of the recommendations because this indicates that the recommendations are feasible and practical.

This section, then, answers the questions *Who will do it?*, *How will it be done?* and *When?* To answer these questions you will need to consider the issues of:

- *resources* (physical, financial and human)
- *timing and sequencing* (when and in what order should things be done?)
- *responsibility* (who is responsible for ensuring that it happens?)
- *measurement* (how will the success, or otherwise, of this recommendation be measured?)

- *possible interventions from the external environment* (will the competition react to this proposal and how will that affect its success? Similarly, how will the government react, if at all, and are there any legal ramifications of the proposal?).

This section needs to be convincingly argued, both to the organisation depicted in the case study and to the marker. Figure 4.5 itemises some of the implementation issues that need to be considered from the sample scenario. *Note:* These are in point form only; in *your* case report they should be expanded and discussed fully.

Spend time ensuring the quality of your case write-ups. Allow at least three to four weeks, if possible. It is very obvious to the marker if you have not spent time on your analysis. Last-minute, all-night efforts will be destined to achieve poor results.

- Arrange for Marilyn to be:
  - (a) counselled for stress
  - (b) counselled for her leadership style
  - (c) given immediate mentoring support.

The costs of these counselling programs are likely to be less than those involving recruitment and selection of a new staff member. If Marilyn will not agree, point out the alternatives, with loss of her employment as one option.

- Arrange for a consultant to assist the workgroup using group dynamics.

- Prepare a position paper on the benefits to management of quality service processes.

- Include project timeline and costs. Estimate the benefits to the company.

FIGURE 4.5   Implementation

Think in terms of a highly paid, busy senior executive reading this report. You need to get your arguments across forcefully and not waste time setting the scene or transmitting information the reader already knows or that has little or no relevance to the problems identified. Do not waste your words on re-presenting the case information, only focus on important facts or items of interest; assume your reader is familiar with the case details. In addition, readers will probably not want to spend much time flipping through appendices, so the body of your report will need to stand alone. It is also likely that in the 'real world', a busy executive would engage other analysts to examine your calculations and appendices carefully, so make sure they are accurate and well prepared.

As you can see, the case analysis process requires you to anchor the case in time and identify critical points that enable you to analyse and filter the information towards achieving a set of recommendations and a viable implementation plan.

So there needs to be a clear thread from the start of the case report to the end, where your recommendations and implementation plans are logically related to your problems and analysis.

4.4 Strategic analysis tools

Section 4.2 mentioned two strategic analysis tools that could greatly assist your case study preparation: the situation analysis and the SWOT analysis. Although these are optional tools, some courses require the use of one, or both, as evidence in the analysis. Check your course guidelines to see if these tools are specific requirements for the case analysis you are conducting. These tools are now discussed in more detail.

4.4.1   The SWOT analysis

A SWOT analysis requires you to identify the firm's strengths and weaknesses, as well as the external environmental opportunities and threats (see figure 4.6). If you do make use of either a situation analysis or a SWOT analysis, make sure you include the results in an appendix to the final report as supporting information.

Strengths	Weaknesses	Opportunities	Threats
✓	✓	✓	✓
✓	✓	✓	✓
✓	✓	✓	✓
✓	✓	✓	✓

FIGURE 4.6   SWOT analysis

4.4.2   Situation analysis

A situation analysis is not an essential item for case analysis, but many students find it a helpful tool. Figure 4.7 shows the situational analysis framework (Payne 1993). You will note that not all the analysis areas suggested will be relevant to every discipline area, and indeed there may be other areas that are important for a particular case. The situation analysis is therefore open to modification. Its main use is to help students make sense of the relationships between areas of importance and to ensure that all areas have been given due consideration.

4.5 Summary

There are two main types of case study that students may encounter. They are:
■ the short case study
■ the Harvard MBA-style case study.

The short case study normally consists of a short description of an organisation or business situation. This type of case study may be used by instructors to provide examples to demonstrate how particular theoretical concepts apply in practical situations. Questions that require students to apply theoretical and analytical skills to provide an answer may also be attached to a case study of this type.

For the longer Harvard MBA-style case study, a more detailed case analysis and subsequent report are generally required.

Environmental analysis

- Political
- Economic
- Social
- Technological
- Financial
- Legal
- Regulatory
- Religious
- Global

Competitive analysis

- Major competitors
- Their goals and objectives
- Marketplace behaviour
- Market share
- Growth
- Service quality
- Positioning
- Operations and resources
- Marketing mix and strategies
- Indirect competitors

Situation analysis

Market analysis

- Size
- Growth
- Customer segments
- Customer needs
- Buyer behaviour
- Intermediaries

Company analysis

- The firm's goals and objectives
- Market share
- Service quality
- Positioning
- Operations and resources
- Marketing mix strategies
- HR policies and procedures

FIGURE 4.7 The situation analysis

Remember that most case reports have drawn on a considerable quantity of research material for their analysis and to develop their recommendations. This material should be placed in an appendix to streamline the report and to reduce the word length. It is important, however, to refer to the material in the appendices in the body of the report, and to summarise the main points or findings of such material. Do not just refer the marker to a particular appendix with no reason or summary of information given in the report.

 Based on the results of the strategic analysis, it can be seen that a diversification strategy will provide Smith Chemicals with the best outcome. This strategy was particularly evident following the identification of the company's weak financial status, combined with increasingly aggressive competition from a number of key players in the industry, and a general decline in market share (see the complete strategic analysis in appendix 3 for more specific details).

Not this:

 Based on the results of the strategic analysis (appendix 3), it can be seen that a diversification strategy will provide Smith Chemicals with the best outcome.

In this chapter, the steps required to prepare a Harvard MBA style case study and the components required in the resulting case study report are discussed in detail. Examples of case analysis techniques and sample report sections are also provided.

4.6 List of references

Lovelock, CH 1991, *Services marketing*, 2nd edn, Prentice Hall, Englewood Cliffs, NJ.

Kashani, K 1992, *Managing global marketing*, PWS Kent, USA.

5 | Essay writing

5.1 Introduction

During your studies at university you may be required to write numerous formal essays. This experience will help you to develop strong written communication skills that are essential in many careers. Essay writing will also help to strengthen your library research skills and to hone your reasoning skills. This is because, in an essay, you will require appropriate reference material to support your argument and will need to weigh up often conflicting evidence in order to reach a conclusion. Essays differ from reports in a number of ways. Specifically, they require a different format or layout and also a different style of writing. An essay requires the writer to argue, defend or justify a point or view with respect to a particular topic or question. To this end, essays require cohesive arguments couched in complete and well-considered sentences and paragraphs. Bullet points and short annotated sentences should be avoided, each new sentence should link to the previous one and each paragraph should link to the next. In report writing, new paragraphs or ideas can often be sequenced with headings whereas in essays, heading are not normally used so each new idea needs to be introduced and then concluded within the paragraph structure. The key stages to writing a formal essay are explored in the following section.

5.2 Selecting the topic

The first step is to select a topic (if given a choice). It is a good idea to be guided in your selection by personal interest but availability of library and other resources should also be taken into account.

5.3 Analysing the topic

Once you have selected the topic, make sure of the essay question's requirements. Look up any unfamiliar words in a dictionary. If the question is based on a term that is contested (that is, where there is no consensus on a definition), you might need to incorporate some discussion about the definition in the essay. For example, if required to 'discuss whether Australia is a democracy', your answer would depend very much on how *democracy* was defined.

Note also what action the instruction verb requires. For example, *discuss* requires a different style of writing from *debate*. Refer to page 137, which outlines some of the more common instruction verbs used in various forms of assessment.

Note any qualifying words or phrases that set limits to your study. If you were asked to 'Evaluate the claim that throughout the 1990s Australian unionism was under siege', you would need to concentrate on a particular location (Australia) during a particular era (the 1990s).

Remember, there is no *one* correct answer to an essay question. Generally, there are many explanations of why things occur and many different, equally defensible viewpoints on a topic. You will need to weigh up the evidence presented for each point of view. Even if you are convinced that a particular position is correct, it is essential to acknowledge opposing arguments and indicate what you perceive to be their failings or weaknesses and why.

5.4 Planning

Once you are sure you know what the question is asking you to do, you can begin planning the essay. This is not an easy task because it is difficult to initiate a plan without knowing much about the topic. Some initial reading may be needed for you to begin formulating ideas. Once the topic has been grasped, the planning can commence. This is an important stage because the plan ensures the material is arranged in a logical way. While a plan is essential, it is also important to recognise that this structure is not fixed rigidly at this stage. Subsequent research may introduce new ideas that need to be incorporated in the original plan. Some students find it helpful to arrange their plan like a table of contents to help them 'see' the logical flow of idea and argument. For example, if writing an essay about the 'Impact of television advertising on the consumption values of children', it would be necessary to firstly discuss what consumption values are and how they relate to children before considering the impact of television on those values. In this sort of question you may also need to limit the scope of your answer to allow you to meet word restrictions. For example, it would be reasonable to assume that television advertising has changed considerably since television was first introduced, and the style, number and focus of advertisements has also changed. To answer this question you might limit your research and discussion to the last 10 years on the basis that this period has seen the most growth in the number of television advertisements directed at children (of course you would have referenced evidence of this assumption). If you do intend to limit or scope your essay, then you need to defend your rationale (with supporting researched evidence) and outline the boundaries of the scope in the introduction paragraph so that the marker knows what you are doing. It is also a good idea to check your assumptions and scope with your examiner before going further to make sure they are happy with your approach.

5.5 Research

You will normally be expected to go beyond the study material provided and the textbook in order to find sufficient material for an essay. Wide reading will provide sufficient breadth of knowledge to make judgements about conflicting points of view. The course instructor will generally provide written guidelines about suitable texts.

Reference lists in relevant books are also useful, as is the library subject index. Librarians are generally willing to help students to find appropriate material (see section 1.5.3). Do not leave your research to the last minute because you might find the material you want has already been borrowed.

Once suitable reference sources have been found, the necessary information should be noted or photocopied and websites copied and bookmarked with access dates noted (remember web based material can change, so a hard copy is also a good idea). The reference material used should be organised or filed in some fashion, especially if the essay is a long one. Make sure detailed records of all relevant reference material are kept so that material can be correctly cited.

 'Post-it' notes are very useful for marking pages of books from which citations will be made. Manila folders, labelled according to theme or topic, are a simple and useful method for organising and storing reference material for long essays or reports.

5.6 Writing the essay

Once the material has been gathered, the writing can begin. An essay must have an *introduction*, a *body* and a *conclusion*. The introduction should tell the reader what to expect. Essays are not mystery stories, in which the reader waits until the end to find out what it has all been about. The introduction should introduce the main theme or argument so that the reader has some idea of what follows. You might find it useful to write the introduction last. You can then ensure it is consistent with the arguments and evidence presented in your essay. The introduction should also generally present the issues you are going to discuss and the order in which they will appear.

When writing an essay it is not normally recommended that headings be used (check your course notes for your particular instructor's view on this). This means that your paragraphs must be well linked and have a logical flow from one idea or point of discussion to the next.

Remember that the first part of each sentence, paragraph and essay has the most impact on the reader's mind, so always express your main idea (rather than parenthetical issues) at the start. For example, the first sentence of a paragraph should be a topic or theme sentence that summarises the main idea that will be developed in the paragraph. Each paragraph should contain one main idea. Avoid one-sentence paragraphs: academic ideas should be complex enough to warrant more than a single sentence to present them. Also avoid long, tortuous sentences that are hard to follow. Try to include a *linker* at the start of each paragraph so the reader can clearly follow your line of thought from paragraph to paragraph (e.g. *Furthermore*, *On the other hand* or *The next step is*). A *summary sentence* at the end of the paragraph or section will also help to clarify your argument.

Your argument should be presented in the body of the essay and be supported by evidence. Make sure that what you write is consistent with and does not contradict the points made in the introduction. Also ensure that related ideas are grouped together in paragraphs and that the final sentence of each provides a link to the next set of related ideas in the following paragraph.

The conclusion should tie together the themes discussed in the essay and spell out their implications. Make sure that the conclusion is consistent with the introduction and with what the question asks. Be aware, too, that the conclusion is not the place to introduce new ideas. Any ideas should be developed and considered in the body of the report, not in the conclusion of the essay.

Students who achieve high marks for their essay will usually have written a number of drafts. It is a good idea to put the essay aside for a day or two before completing the final draft. This allows a more objective assessment of both the arguments presented and the style of writing used.

5.7 Style

For an essay to be effective, ideas must be communicated clearly. If your first language is English, you should already be familiar with the tools of communication. If you are having trouble with communication, you should seek help from your relevant university student services section. Communication skills can be improved by reading as much as possible. In this way, your vocabulary will improve and the patterns of the language will become more familiar.

For essay presentation, see the guidelines for assessment, specifically sections 1.1, 1.2 and 1.3.

Direct quotations from other sources (even if correctly referenced) should not be used to 'write' an essay. They should only be used sparingly to support or *illustrate* points in the argument, not to make them. You should attempt to summarise the quotations and formulate your interpretation of what they mean and how they add to or support your argument and then in your own words use the information to add credibility or justification to your position (remembering that this is called paraphrasing and still needs correct referencing — see chapter 2). Do not leave it to the reader to interpret the meaning or relevance of direct quotations.

As a general rule, headings are not used in formal essays; however, check with your instructor about whether headings are acceptable in the particular circumstances of your assignment. If this is not clearly spelt out, and you cannot reach your instructor, assume headings are not desirable. Some people argue that headings are inappropriate in an essay, while others believe they are useful as signposts that guide the reader (and the writer) through the essay. If you do use headings, do not number them and use them sparingly. Do not forget to write sentences that link each subsection with the next; do not rely on the heading to provide the link.

5.8 Sample essay

The following sample assignment question and essay will illustrate some of the main points made in this chapter. It is based on and, in part, extracted from an essay written by an MBA student.

The following assignment was set for consumer behaviour students:

> Observational learning is an important means of socialisation for children, teenagers and adults. Consider the content of popular prime-time television shows. What are the patterns of behaviour that people may learn as a result of watching prime-time television? What, if any, are the public policy implications of your analysis?

In response to this assignment question, students wrote essays on the impact of observational learning on socialisation in which they examined the ethical and social issues involved in this area in relation to television programming. One student, Lisa, wrote an essay that was particularly well structured and written, and this is an adaptation of her work.

Note that this essay does not include headings, although in many cases this would be permissible. Check with your instructor or the assignment guidelines to determine the ruling on this for your particular assignment.

Observational learning and public policy implications

Observational learning, also known as vicarious or social learning, plays a significant role in the socialisation of individuals (Mowen & Minor 1998). The purpose of this paper is to address the theoretical issues related to observational learning as a mechanism that results in consumer socialisation. In particular, the scope of this paper will be confined to how people learn patterns of behaviour by observing others in prime-time television shows. A discussion of observational learning and the process of socialisation is presented, followed by a review of the patterns of behaviour that may be learned as a result of watching prime-time television shows. Finally, some implications for public policy in this area are presented.

Observational learning has been defined as 'the phenomenon whereby people develop patterns of behaviour by observing the actions of others' (Mowen & Minor 1998, p. 47). This theory identifies two ways in which people's behaviour can be affected. The first is where a person perceives positive consequences resulting from the observed behaviour; they are likely to imitate such behaviour. The second is where a person perceives negative consequences of an observed behaviour; they are likely to attempt to avoid such behaviour (Assael 1995). In this manner the theory of observational

[Margin note 1:] Selection of her topic was important to Lisa. She chose to write about this topic from a range of topics because she was interested in it and was able to find suitable references.

[Margin note 2:] Lisa's introduction tells the reader how she has interpreted the topic and how the essay is structured. Now the reader knows what to expect. Note also she has provided information on the scope and boundaries of her essay.

learning incorporates both the principles of cognitive learning, where people are anticipating consequences of actions, and the principles of operant conditioning — where reinforcement is shown to shape behaviour (Mowen & Minor 1998). It is these learning mechanisms that are known to contribute to the process of socialisation.

Socialisation is defined as 'the process by which individuals acquire the knowledge, skills and dispositions that enable them to participate as members of society' (Mowen & Minor 1998, p. 534). From a consumer behaviour perspective, socialisation refers to how people acquire skills, knowledge and attitudes that enable them to function as consumers in the marketplace (Assael 1995; Schiffman et al. 1997). Children, specifically, learn consumption skills as part of the socialisation process from interaction with family members, peers and the media, particularly the persuasive influence of television (Craig-Lees et al. 1995; Schiffman et al. 1997; Mowen & Minor 1998). Prime-time television, in particular, has the ability to influence much behaviour, both positively and negatively, due to its wide reach. Children are most vulnerable to this form of persuasion, as will be shown next. ◄——

Note the strong link from this paragraph to the next. The reader is led into the paragraph expecting to read about children and persuasion.

It is well known that prior to a child developing abstract thought, which occurs at about the age of ten, they are particularly vulnerable to advertising messages and the seductive appeal of television reality (Craig-Lees et al. 1995; Schiffman et al. 1997; Mowen & Minor 1998). Children (and others) learn by observing the patterns and consequences of behaviours of television actors in simulated television realities and use these as guides for their own consumption and social behaviours. Prime-time television shows are well known for containing story-lines that include subtle product marketing messages, as well as behavioural modelling scenarios (Schiffman 1997). This has particular relevance for marketers in developing promotional strategies aimed at children in particular.

In spite of the obvious implications for observational learning in the socialisation of children, socialisation is an ongoing process and is not strictly confined to childhood, although it is more intense for those at an earlier age (Loudon & Della Bitta 1993). Teenagers and adults also are continually undergoing further socialisation as their reference groups, social settings and circumstances change. This means that there is potential to influence consumption behaviour through many stages of a person's life. Interestingly, in relation to consumption it is noted that observational learning through socialisation of the family has the greatest influence on the rational aspects of consumption, while learning through observation from television and the media influences the emotional aspects of consumption (Assael 1995).

Each key idea that Lisa introduces is appropriately referenced.

The general patterns of behaviour that people learn from viewing prime-time television shows can be both positive and negative. Negative behaviours such as insolence, disrespect for elders, a dislike of learning and even aggression may come from shows such as *South Park*, *The Simpsons*, most sporting programs and even, to some degree, *Neighbours* and *Home and away*. Positive behaviours such as helping, good parenting skills, caring for friends and telling the truth may come from shows like *The Pretender*, *Blue heelers*, *Home improvements*, *Friends* and *Seinfeld*. Television is a useful medium for developing desired modelling scenarios where people engage in certain behaviours and subsequently receive reinforcement (Loudon & Della Bitta 1993) — for example a sit-com which shows someone telling the truth about a transgression and instead of being punished, they are rewarded for their honesty. Television also has the ability to engage in product marketing at both an obvious level (shows such as *Burke's backyard* and *Bright ideas*) and at a less obvious level (such as when the stars of *Friends* go to a Hootie and the Blowfish concert) (Mowen & Minor 1998).

The effect of prime-time television shows engaging in product marketing has implications for public policy, particularly in relation to the impact on children. The greater the exposure children have to television, the greater the probability that they will accept the images and associations observed (Assael 1995; Shiffman et al. 1997). This is particularly critical when it is known that for the majority of children younger than nine years, television is their principal source of marketplace information (Craig-Lees et al. 1995). It is for this reason that many countries, including Australia, have begun to regulate the content and timing of television advertising and programming. In spite of this, recent research has suggested that parents and friends still have a greater influence over children's product choices than does television advertising, although the friends most likely get their information from television (O'Shannessy 1994; Moschis 1985; Childers & Akshay 1992).

Here Lisa is developing her argument and supporting her views with researched evidence.

This regulation of television content and advertising is both a government and an industry initiative through legislation and the Federation of Australian Commercial Television Stations (FACTS). There is also more advertising of the existence of such regulatory bodies and of the rights of television watchers in an attempt to better inform the marketplace and to empower them into becoming more involved consumers.

Consumers who are more aware of their rights are less likely to be subjected to unethical practices, which has been the criticism of many in relation to the use of product marketing on prime-time television (Mowen & Minor 1998). The complete embargo of the use of product marketing is not a feasible option for policy makers, so their best course of action is to focus on consumer education using the same principles of observational learning on their target audiences.

In summary, observational learning has been shown to be an important learning mechanism for the socialisation of consumers. It is directly through observation that many consumers learn the appropriate consumption behaviours and social norms of our society. Prime-time television shows provide viewers with access to 'real life' scenarios that consumers use to match and modify their own behaviours to, and in this regard they can be open to misuse by unethical marketers. Whether obvious or subtle, product marketing in television shows can add authenticity to a product because a consumer is less likely to discount the message, and this is particularly true in the case of young children (Mowen & Minor 1998). By understanding this socialisation process, public policy makers, through implementing both regulation and educational programs, are able to ensure that consumers are not unfairly or unethically treated by unscrupulous marketers.

In her conclusion, Lisa ties the points in her discussion together. She finishes with an interesting and supported statement that confirms her initial suggestion that observational learning helps in the development of public policy for advertising.

References

Assael, H 1995, *Consumer behaviour and marketing action*, 5th edn, South-Western College Publishing, Ohio.

Childers, TL & Akshay, RR 1992, 'The influence of familial and peer-based reference groups on consumer decisions', *Journal of Consumer Research*, vol. 19, no. 2, pp. 472–85.

Lisa has been careful to list all the material she has referenced in her essay (though all are not shown here).

5.9 Summary

An essay is another distinctive form of written communication. An essay writer is required to argue, defend or justify a point or view with respect to a particular topic or question. Essays differ from reports both in format and in the style of writing used.

The use of headings within essays is contentious. Some say that headings are inappropriate in essays and interfere with the flow of argument. Others contend that headings provide useful signposts for the reader. The use of headings, appropriate writing styles for essays, how to analyse an essay topic, how to research essay topics and other useful hints for writing essays have been detailed in this chapter. A sample essay has also been included to illustrate the main issues discussed in the chapter.

5.10 Some variations on the formal essay structure

At times you will be asked to present assignments in forms other than 'formal' essays. You should read the instructions for these very carefully and note specifically any deviations from the formal essay format described here. Such variations will relate primarily to the use of headings and subheadings. Terms used by instructors to describe such modified essays may include *critical essays*, *critical discussion*, *comprehensive analysis* or simply *discussion*.

6 | Oral presentations

6.1 Overview

The ability to deliver oral presentations competently and confidently is a skill that is vital for every contemporary business professional. Even the best ideas can be lost if they are not communicated effectively to others.

One important factor that sets oral communication apart from written communication is *immediacy*. Written communication offers authors the opportunity to revise their work continually, until they are satisfied that their message is clear and concise, before delivering the finished work to the reader. The reader can then absorb the message at leisure, reviewing the material as many times as is required to understand the author's point of view fully. In oral communication, the presenter usually has only one chance to deliver the message to the audience and, unless the presentation is recorded, the audience gets only one chance to comprehend the message.

When delivering an oral presentation, it is, therefore, very important that the speaker uses what might be his or her only chance to convey a message as effectively as possible.

Many very useful sources of information are available on delivering oral presentations. Students should refer to these for detailed information. The guidelines here provide a useful starting point for developing effective presentations.

6.2 Oral presentations at university

Simply reading about how to deliver good oral presentations is not sufficient to make someone into a good presenter. The essential component in developing good oral communication skills is practice. During a student's study at university, many opportunities are provided to practise and develop oral communication skills. This may involve simply taking part in informal discussions during tutorial sessions and at residential schools or could involve actually delivering a formal presentation that forms a component of a student's assessment.

Sometimes, students may be asked to prepare oral presentations on tape. The following guidelines will assist not only in the preparation of oral presentations, but will also provide an indication of the points that will be considered by those assessing the quality of student presentations.

Oral delivery of any formal presentation involves three main stages:

- preparing the presentation
- delivering the presentation
- handling questions from the audience.

6.3 Preparing the presentation

Preparation is the most important stage in any formal presentation.

The objectives

The first step in preparing a presentation is to decide:

- the purpose of the presentation (i.e. what you wish to achieve)
- who the audience will be.

Purpose of the presentation

The primary purpose of most oral presentations is to entertain, persuade or inform.

Most formal business presentations tend to fall into the latter two categories (i.e. to persuade or inform). The objective of a presentation designed primarily to *inform* an audience is to deliver the information as accurately and efficiently as possible. In contrast, a presentation designed to *persuade* an audience will seek to influence the beliefs or attitudes of the audience in some way (e.g. to 'sell' a product or idea). The purpose of the presentation must be clearly determined before starting to create the presentation. Having a clear idea of the purpose will assist the presenter in deciding on both the content of the presentation and the most effective presentation method.

Audience

The presenter should try to find out as much as possible about the audience before starting to create the presentation. The following questions may assist in analysing the audience:

- What will the audience be expecting from the presentation?
- How much do they already know about the topic of the presentation?

- Will they be receptive or hostile to the information presented in the topic?

- Is the audience composed of technical or non-technical people?

- Are there any sensitive issues (e.g. political or cultural) that should be avoided for this audience?

- How much time does the audience have? (What is the cost of its time?)

- What standard of dress should be adopted for delivery of the presentation?

In summary, the presentation, regardless of the audience, needs to be: (a) concise and informative; and (b) free of technical jargon and of tedious explanations of complex and esoteric issues.

Timing

The presentation should be timed carefully. If it is too short, there is a risk that the presenter will miss the opportunity to deliver adequately his or her well-researched and innovative ideas. In contrast, overly long presentations can be both ineffective and discourteous. They may not only become boring for the audience, but also could impact upon the time allocated to speakers that follow.

6.3.1 Presentation venue

It is important in the early stages of preparing for the presentation to learn as much about the presentation venue as possible. Information on such things as the size of the room and the facilities available will help the presenter to decide on the best approach to presenting his or her information. For example, many presenters like to use electronic presentation equipment but may discover that the venue does not provide the required facilities. Overhead transparencies, which are becoming increasingly less common today, require different preparation and presentation techniques, but might be the only alternative should computerised presentation equipment not be available.

It is also important to arrive at the venue early. This enables the presenter to check that the equipment is functioning correctly and that, for example, compatible versions of any software packages that are to be used are available.

6.3.2 Structure of the presentation

Formal oral presentations must be well structured to be effective. Their structure is very similar to formal written documents in that they are made up of:

- an introduction

- a body

- a conclusion.

As the old adage says, 'Tell them what you're going to tell them, tell them, and tell them what you've told them'.

6.3.3 Introduction and conclusion

The main purpose of the introduction is for the speaker to introduce himself or herself, to establish a rapport with the audience and to introduce the main points that will be covered in the body of the presentation. (Sometimes a session presenter will introduce the speaker before the presentation begins.)

The purpose of the conclusion is to summarise and re-emphasise the main points of the presentation. If the objective of the presentation is to persuade the audience, then the conclusion is the place to reinforce in the minds of the audience exactly what action should be taken. The audience will then leave with that thought uppermost in their minds. The conclusion is, therefore, a very important component of the presentation and should not be neglected.

Preparation of the introduction and conclusion should normally be left until after the main body of the presentation has been created to ensure that every aspect of the presentation has been addressed. As a general rule, the introduction and conclusion should each occupy approximately 10 per cent of the presentation.

6.3.4 Body of the presentation

The body of the presentation should also be structured and presented in a logical sequence. The easiest way to prepare the body of the presentation is as follows:

1 Write down or highlight (an outliner in a word processing program can be a useful tool) all of the main points to be covered during the presentation. These will be the major 'signposts' in the presentation. (If presenting in a team, topics may be divided among the team members.)
2 Decide on appropriate subtopics within each of the main points chosen.
3 The library, or other information sources, can now be used with a clear idea of the material that must be researched to complete the body of the presentation.

Using this approach achieves two objectives: first, it imposes a natural structure on the presentation and second, it helps to ensure the major issues are not overlooked. Some research may be needed before step 1 if the topic of the presentation is unfamiliar to the presenter.

When creating the body of the presentation, it is also worth noting that using simple analogies can often help to convey an idea or message quickly and effectively to the audience. For example, using a well-known organisation or an event that has been discussed in the newspapers recently can help to illustrate a point. It is, therefore, worth spending time thinking about the most effective way to convey the message.

6.3.5 Visual aids

Sight plays a major role in our ability to absorb information. Most readers will be familiar with the saying 'A picture is worth a thousand words'. Well-designed visual aids provide a useful complement to most presentations for the following reasons:

■ They can be used to reinforce what is being said.

■ They can help maintain audience interest and concentration.

■ They can be used to illustrate concepts that are difficult to explain verbally.

■ They are a useful prompt for the presenter.

Traditionally, visual aids were created using overhead transparencies but today electronic presentation techniques using computer packages such as Microsoft PowerPoint are more common. Computer-based presentation software is discussed in more detail in section 6.6 of this chapter.

Irrespective of the presentation medium used, visual aids must be well designed, otherwise they can detract from the overall effectiveness of the presentation. The following points should be kept in mind when preparing visual aids:

- Make sure the slides are not too cluttered; use large fonts (24-point is recommended).

- Use a mixture of upper- and lower-case letters and present one major topic per slide.

- Include a maximum of seven points per slide.

- Make sure the slides can be read easily by everyone in the audience.

- Make use of diagrams or graphics where possible, rather than using a lot of text.

- If using diagrams or graphs, keep them simple and uncluttered.

- Use colour if possible, but sparingly and appropriately (no more than three or four different colours on the one slide). Choose foreground and background colour combinations that allow any text to be read easily by the audience.

- Ensure that all slides follow a consistent style (i.e. the topic in the same spot on every slide, a similar background on each slide etc.). This makes it easier for the audience to follow.

- Do not use too many slides (no more than one every five minutes).

6.3.6 Audience handouts

Handouts are useful, particularly when the presenter seeks to persuade the audience, both during (to reinforce the information being presented) and after the presentation. Generally, handouts will contain a list of the major points being discussed in the presentation and perhaps a summary of the main message of the presentation. This type of handout should be distributed before the presentation, although some people suggest that this can distract the audience from what you are saying. If the audience is likely to want to take notes about your presentation, then handing out information first is a good idea.

If the presentation requires the review of very detailed or voluminous information, it is usually better to summarise the information verbally during the presentation and to provide more detailed information in handouts for the audience. These handouts should be distributed afterwards so that the audience is not distracted during the presentation. To draw attention to the handouts, the presenter should mention them at an appropriate point during the presentation.

6.3.7 Practising the presentation

To perform at their very best on the day, sportsmen and women must practise their skills before the event. The same principal applies when preparing for a formal presentation. Presenters should deliver their presentation at least once (preferably twice), as though they were presenting it to a live audience. Having someone there to provide a critique of the practice presentation is also helpful (this is easier if presenting as a member of a team).

Practice is important for a number of reasons:

- It instills confidence in the presenter.
- It will reveal whether the presentation will fit into the time allowed (not too long or too short).
- It provides a 'testing ground' for the visual aids (are they too small or too cluttered?).
- If presenting in a team, transitions from one speaker to the next can be practised.
- In some cases it can provide the opportunity to experience first hand, the venue in which the real presentation will take place. Importantly, this will provide the opportunity to practise in, and become familiar with, the actual equipment and the room or auditorium.

6.3.8 Planning for contingencies

It is important to plan for possible unexpected events on the day of the presentation. For example, if the presentation time is unexpectedly reduced, which parts could be omitted without interrupting the flow?

Presenters should plan for possible equipment failure. What happens if the computer system that is to be used for the presentation fails two minutes before the presentation is due to start? A possible solution to this problem is to have overhead transparencies prepared as a backup.

The presenter should also try to anticipate possible questions from the audience and prepare answers accordingly. If presenting in a team, it should be decided beforehand whether one person will act as the spokesperson who answers all the questions or whether each team member will answer questions on one particular aspect of the presentation.

6.3.9 Just before the presentation

It is wise to arrive at the venue at least 30 minutes before the presentation is due to start. This will allow plenty of time to ensure that the seating arrangements for the audience are appropriate and the equipment is functioning correctly. It will also provide some time to overcome any anxiety experienced by the presenter.

6.3.10 Equipment

Presenters should ensure that any equipment required for the presentation is set up and functioning correctly and that the instructions for operating the equipment and lighting in the room are understood. This applies in particular to complicated computer and audiovisual equipment. Last-minute equipment failure can be a disaster for the presenter who has not anticipated it.

6.3.11 Anxiety

Most people experience a degree of anxiety when faced with making a public presentation. This is natural, but uncontrolled nervousness can detract from an otherwise good presentation. At this point, presenters should already have taken the first two steps towards controlling anxiety: *preparation* and *practice*. Being prepared, having a good knowledge of the content of the presentation and knowing that it will work because it has been practised will instill confidence and help to reduce nervousness.

At this stage, presenters who are still nervous should take a few deep breaths (trying not to hyperventilate). This will help to release tension. Another useful relaxation technique is to gradually tense every muscle in the body, starting from the feet through to the neck, arms and hands, then slowly release the tension and take a deep breath. Doing this once or twice should help presenters to feel more relaxed.

6.4 Delivering the presentation

6.4.1 Delivery speed

When delivering presentations it is important to avoid speaking too quickly. Generally, the speed of the presentation should be slower than the speed of normal conversation. The presenter should monitor their presentation speed as the presentation progresses. This will help to ensure that they are not jumbling words or skimming over topics so quickly that the audience loses the point of the presentation, or speaking so slowly that the audience becomes bored or loses interest.

6.4.2 Gestures

Natural gestures will add a further dimension to presentations. Anxiety can sometimes cause gestures to be stiff and unnatural. However, as the presentation progresses and the presenter feels more comfortable, it is often easier to use gestures more naturally. Whether gestures are used at all is entirely optional. Actions that should definitely be avoided include folding arms, putting hands in pockets or nervously wringing hands. These gestures can be very distracting for the audience.

6.4.3 Audience rapport

During the presentation it is very important for each member of the audience to feel as though he or she is being addressed personally. One method that will help to establish a rapport with the audience is to maintain eye contact. If presenting to a small group, the presenter should try to focus on each person for approximately one to three seconds before moving on to the next. If presenting to a large group of people, maintaining eye contact with each individual becomes very difficult. In this case, a useful technique is to select small groups of people in the audience and focus on someone within each group before moving on to the next group. In this way, despite the distance between speaker and audience, each member of the audience will still feel as though he or she is being addressed personally.

Focusing just above the back row and scanning the eyes across a large auditorium is another technique that will help to achieve this result.

6.4.4 Reading the speech

In some cases, reading a speech in its entirety is necessary. However, in general, reading a presentation is not acceptable. When a speech is read, maintaining eye contact with the audience becomes much more difficult; it is, therefore, much harder to maintain the audience's attention. Should it be necessary to read a speech, the speaker should pause from time to time to scan the members of the audience as a means of addressing this issue.

Rote-learning a speech is also not a good practice to adopt. This can tend to make the speech sound stilted. Nervousness can also cause memory lapses, the result of which could be uncomfortable and embarrassing silences. Using notes or presentation slides as prompts is a much better approach to adopt.

6.4.5 Stance during the speech

The presenter should not slouch or stand too stiffly. It is best to adopt a relaxed, upright posture, with the weight evenly distributed to both legs. If available, a lectern should be used. A lectern provides a place for presentation notes, as well as somewhere for the presenter to rest his or her hands (and somewhere to hide shaking knees!).

When delivering a presentation, it is important to try not to stand with feet fixed in one spot. Continually pacing backwards and forwards is not acceptable either, since it can be distracting for the audience. An occasional step towards the audience can help to emphasise a point and help to maintain attention. Moving about a little during the presentation can also help to relieve tension.

6.4.6 Humour

Humour can be useful in establishing and maintaining a rapport with the audience but should be used wisely, otherwise the presenter risks alienating the audience. Presenters should take care to:

- Avoid humour that could offend any member of the audience.
- Establish a link between any humourous anecdotes used and the speaker, topic, audience or occasion.
- Avoid using humour unless confident that it will be well received by the audience and will enhance the presentation.

6.4.7 Nervousness

Nervous presenters should avoid actions such as holding up pieces of paper. Shaking paper can very effectively communicate nervousness to the audience. Having a glass of water nearby is also a good idea. A dry mouth can cause the presenter to start coughing or, at best, reduce the ability to effectively project their voice.

6.4.8 Annoying habits

The presenter should try to avoid *ums*, *ahs* and *errs* in his or her address, along with actions such as continually tapping the feet, or drumming a pointer or pen on the lectern. These, often subconscious manifestations of nervousness, can become most annoying for the audience and risk distracting attention from the speaker's message.

6.4.9 Presenting in teams

Presenting in teams is, on one hand, less stressful for each individual team member because others are there to share the responsibility. On the other hand, if the team does not work well together during the presentation this can be very distracting for the audience.

Co-presenters should carry out the following steps to ensure they work well together and that the presentation flows smoothly from beginning to end:

- Decide before the presentation which presenters will deliver which parts of the presentation.
- Practise the presentation as a team before delivering it on the day.
- Decide before the presentation how questions will be answered and which team members will be responsible for answering questions after the presentation.
- Introduce each team member during the introduction, and tell the audience which aspect of the topic each speaker will address.
- As the presentation passes from one speaker to the next, the former should introduce the latter and briefly remind the audience which aspect that speaker will address.

It is also important that, if presenting in a team, all team members participate.

6.5 Handling questions from the audience

In most cases, time will be allocated after the presentation for questions from the audience. The person answering audience questions should:

- Clarify and summarise questions that are verbose.
- Restate all questions to ensure everyone in the audience has heard them (unless the group is very small).
- If unable to answer a particular question, be honest and say so. They should also indicate that an answer will be found and relayed to the person asking the question.

6.6 Computer-based presentation software

6.6.1 Preplanning

Earlier sections of this chapter discuss general points that should be considered when creating and delivering oral presentations. These points are relevant irrespective of what visual aids are used to help the speaker communicate the message to the audience.

This section focuses on computer-based presentation software tools. This type of tool has many advantages over other traditional visual aids such as overhead transparencies or 35 mm slides. One of the most important advantages is flexibility. For example, presentations created using presentation software tools can be changed at the last minute or can be easily tailored to suit a number of different audiences. This type of software also allows the person creating the presentation to incorporate colour, animation, sound and video into the presentation to make it more stimulating to the audience.

Computer-based presentation software can be a very powerful communication tool but many factors must be considered to produce an effective final product. The process of creating an effective presentation consists of the following stages:

- deciding how the presentation will be used
- creating the presentation
- rehearsing the presentation
- delivering the presentation.

6.6.2 How will the presentation be used?

The first step in creating a presentation is to ask the question *What is the purpose of the presentation?* This will determine the approach used to create the presentation and will also determine what features will need to be incorporated into the final product for it to be effective.

Presentations can be broadly categorised as those that are delivered:

- to a constantly changing audience
- as an interactive presentation
- in conjunction with an oral presentation.

The first type is one that will be used to convey information to an audience that is constantly changing. This type of audience might be found at, for example, a trade show. In this situation, the presentation should be completely self-contained. It may also incorporate synchronised commentary and video clips to enhance the overall interest and capture the audience's attention. Usually, it will be configured to run in a continuous loop so that once the end of the presentation is reached it will automatically recommence from the start. This is so that people who have arrived after the start of the presentation will have the opportunity to see all of the information being presented.

Another type of presentation is one in which the audience (usually a single person) can choose what information is presented by clicking on navigation buttons located on each slide or screen within the presentation. An information kiosk or an intranet site would be a typical application of this sort of presentation. These require careful design to ensure that the person viewing the presentation can easily find specific information and also navigate through the entire presentation without missing important information.

The final type of presentation is one in which a speaker stands in front of an audience and delivers an oral presentation using a computer-based presentation tool to enhance the overall communication process. This type of presentation occurs commonly in business and is the primary focus of this section. *Note:* this section discusses generic features found in most presentation software packages.

6.6.3 Creating the presentation

Because of the rich multimedia toolkit available in most presentation software packages, it is tempting first to incorporate every possible feature into a presentation and second to start by adding all of the multimedia content before deciding on what information is to be presented and in what order. Neither is a good idea.

By attempting to use every possible feature, the presentation may end up being very 'busy' and could ultimately distract the audience from the central theme or message being presented. So it is best to err on the side of simplicity when it comes to including 'sparkle' such as colour, graphics, sound and animation in a presentation. This is discussed in more detail later in the section.

Also, if the 'sparkle' is added before the text, the presentation may end up lacking overall structure, the information content may be disjointed and the audience may be forced to jump backwards and forwards from one topic to another. Therefore, it is wise to start by deciding what the information content and structure will be before adding the multimedia content when creating any presentation.

6.6.3.1 Using the outline view

The first step is to identify the broad structure of the presentation. One way to achieve this is to decide on the theme or key messages that the presentation is intended to convey to the audience.

Then the outline view provided by most presentation software can be used to identify the main points in the presentation. Sub-points can be added under the main points, further points can be added under the sub-points, and so on as the presentation content evolves. Using this approach, ideas can be collected and arranged and the presentation can be built with structure, clearly and logically.

Once the structure of the presentation is complete, the software can be used to convert each main point on the outline to an individual slide featuring that point, with the text of the main point being the title of the slide. The relevant sub-points then become bullet points on the slide, with lower-level information appearing under each of the bullet points for that slide.

The advantages of using the outline view to start creating a presentation are:

■ Only text is visible in this view so that the information content is not cluttered with extraneous material such as graphics; therefore, the overall structure of the presentation is clearly visible.

■ The software allows the creator to very easily rearrange information. Points can be 'promoted' or 'demoted', that is, raised to a higher or reduced to a lower level of importance with the click of a button.

- Points (or sections) of the presentation can be moved to other locations or deleted, by highlighting the relevant section in the outline view and either dragging the information to the desired destination or pressing the delete key to remove unwanted information.

- The outline can be converted automatically into individual slides with titles and structured bullet points.

6.6.3.2 Creating a consistent presentation using master slides

It is very important to maintain consistency within a visual presentation. The slide's background, font size, type and colour and the position of repeated information such as slide numbers, should be generally consistent from slide to slide. In some situations it is appropriate to deviate from the standard. Different font sizes, colours or background can be used on particular slides within the overall presentation to create a visual impact where it is necessary to emphasise a particular point. However, this technique should be used sparingly. Too many changes throughout the presentation can cause the audience to become confused.

A feature that is available in most presentation software packages is the *slide master*. This slide is used as a template for the rest of the slides in the presentation and will allow the presentation creator to easily maintain consistency among the slides in the presentation.

Font size, type and colour can be defined on the slide master for each of the bullet point levels in the presentation. For example, the presentation creator may define level 1 bullet text as being *Times New Roman 14 point* and level 2 bullet text as being *Times New Roman 12 point* on the slide master. Then if a level 2 point is added to a presentation slide, its text will be formatted automatically as 12-point Times New Roman. If level 1 text is demoted on the presentation slide to level 2, the font also will change automatically from 14-point Times New Roman to 12-point Times New Roman.

Background colours can be defined on the slide master. Company logos and other graphics can be incorporated. Special slide number and date fields can also be added to the footer. Then when any new slide is added to the presentation, attributes that have been included on the slide master will be incorporated into the new slide. Dates and slide numbers will be generated automatically.

Apart from font type, size and colour, background colour and pattern, it is also important to maintain consistency in how paragraphs are formatted, how dates are presented and how numbers are presented within the presentation. This makes it much easier for the audience to identify and comprehend the information being presented.

Another important consideration is to make sure that both the font colour and font size of the text being used in the presentation are appropriate in terms of visibility. For example, light green fonts on a light blue background can be very difficult to read. On the other hand, a white font on a dark blue background is usually clear and easy to read. It is also generally pleasing to the eye. Some colours can clash when used in combination.

A colour's appearance can vary greatly from one computer monitor to the next or between a computer monitor and a projector. Because of this, a presentation that looks good on one computer monitor may not look right or may be difficult to read on another. This is particularly important when using diagrams in a presentation with particular colours to denote particular information. Any problems of this nature can be identified in the rehearsal stage, which is discussed later in this section.

Slide masters are particularly useful for maintaining consistency among the slides in a presentation. Another major advantage is flexibility. If the creator decides, for example that a different background colour would be more appropriate or that the main font size is too large or too small, a whole presentation can be altered very easily by changing the Slide master. All of the slides in the presentation will then change accordingly. This can represent a huge time saving, particularly if there are a large number of slides in the presentation.

6.6.3.3 Speaker notes

It is not wise to clutter slides with too much information. A slide containing a number of easily read bullet points and, perhaps, a large, clear diagram or graphic is better than one with lines and lines of small, hard-to-read text. However, it is important for the presenter to have all of the supporting information in an easily accessible format so that it can be referenced when necessary.

A handy feature provided by most presentation software is the *notes page*. This allows the presenter to enter supplementary information into each slide in the presentation. The information will not be presented to the audience but can be printed out by the presenter to act as a prompt during the presentation. Normally the page will consist of a representation of the slide in the upper half of the page and the accompanying notes in the lower half of the page.

A good time to enter notes into the presentation is when creating each slide. Examples of information that might be recorded include statistics relating to the information on the slide, references to where the information being presented on the slide was sourced and humorous or interesting information that might increase the audience's understanding of the points being discussed.

6.6.3.4 Adding the 'sparkle'

Once the main textual content and structure of the presentation is complete, multi-media content can then be included to improve the presentation.

Illustrations can aid understanding of complex topics. Most presentation packages include tools to draw lines, boxes, circles, curves and arrows. These can be used creatively to illustrate the information content with diagrams. Clip art can also be added, as can graphs to simplify complex numeric content. Care should be exercised though, to ensure that all material used is cleared for copyright before being used for public presentation.

Slide transitions and animation can also add a professional touch to presentations. Many software packages allow slides to be configured so that main points are revealed progressively by clicking on a mouse. Another common feature is transitions. The presentation can be configured so that, for example, when moving from one slide to the next, an image will gradually fade and be replaced by the next slide image.

Sound and video can also be included in presentations, as can links to web-based content.

Presentations can also be set up to run automatically. However, timing is critical for this type of presentation. Information should neither be presented too slowly nor too quickly. If the speed is too slow, the audience may become bored. Presenting information too quickly may mean that slower readers become confused or miss important information. It is also not a particularly good idea to have an automatic presentation if it is to be run in conjunction with a live presentation. It is very difficult for a speaker to keep pace with this type of presentation. When using a computer-based presentation in conjunction with a live speaker it is always best for the speaker to control the speed of the presentation manually by using a mouse or a remote control to advance each slide.

Presenters now have the tools that facilitate the creation of presentations rich in interesting multimedia content. However, it is very important to remember that anything that is added other than the basic message of the presentation must always enhance the message and not detract from it. Audience members should not leave the presentation thinking 'Wow, that was a great spectacle . . . but what did it all mean?' If the audience is left with that impression, then the presenter has failed to deliver an effective presentation.

6.6.3.5 Audience handouts
Most presentation software packages provide a facility for presenters to generate audience handouts to accompany the presentation. These will include an image of the slide and some additional space for the audience member to make notes. Commonly the presenter can format the handout as one, two, four or six slides per page depending on the presentation content and length of the presentation. However, the more slides per page, the harder it is for the information on the handout to be read.

Some presenters prefer to distribute handouts after the presentation and some opt to allow the audience access to the handouts before the presentation commences. Each approach has its advantages and disadvantages. For example, if people have access to the handouts before the presentation, there will be opportunities to make notes as the presentation progresses, but this may distract some people from concentrating on the presenter. Therefore, the choice of whether to distribute handouts before or after the presentation is entirely up to the presenter. However, actual creation of the handouts is a very simple process.

6.6.4 Rehearsing the presentation
It is vital when using electronic presentation technology to rehearse the presentation at least once before the final performance. If possible, it is best to use

the actual equipment that will be used for the presentation to ensure that the presenter has complete familiarity with the equipment. There is nothing more distracting than a presenter who cannot get the equipment to work before or during the presentation.

Among other things, rehearsal will help the presenter to ensure that:

- The projector works properly with the laptop or desktop computer that will be used for the presentation.

- The presenter has appropriate access to computers, projector cabinets and other equipment required for the presentation.

- The projector has a bulb that is functional.

- The colours that are used in the presentation present as expected.

- The text is large enough that it can be read easily from all parts of the room.

- If sound is required, that there are speakers and that they have sufficient volume to be heard throughout the room.

- Remote controls and pointers are functional and do not need battery replacement.

- Spelling and grammar in the presentation are correct.

- Slide transitions and timing are appropriate.

- Any connections with the Internet that are required actually work.

- The presenter is familiar with any keyboard shortcuts that may be required during the presentation (e.g. how to choose a particular slide or go to a previous slide in the presentation).

- The room is sufficiently large to hold the expected audience.

- People can see both the screen and the presenter from all parts of the room.

Well-prepared presenters use rehearsals to identify and correct any potential problems that may prevent the best possible performance on the day. The importance of this stage increases greatly if the presenter is a novice or if they are unfamiliar with the venue or the equipment to be used.

Backups are also important. A backup on a memory stick or CD-ROM and a hard-copy printout may never be required but if something does go wrong with the equipment on the day, they can save a lot of embarrassment.

It is not possible to prepare for every contingency. However, a thorough rehearsal can help to ensure that everything runs smoothly on the day of the presentation.

6.6.5 Delivering the presentation

It is common to see presenters who read every word from the presentation screen (and sometimes actually face the screen). This can soon become extremely boring for the audience. The points on the screen should be used as a prompt to the presenter and to reinforce important points in the audience members' minds, not as an autocue.

Another mistake that some presenters make is to click through slides at lightning speed. This can result either from nervousness or from poor preparation and an attempt by the presenter to get through too much information in too short a time. This is very distracting for the audience and will almost certainly ensure that most will lose concentration very quickly.

Infra-red pointers can be very effective devices when used properly and in an appropriate setting. They are devices that shine an intense red dot onto the screen and can be used by presenters to emphasise particular points of interest during the presentation. They are particularly useful in venues with very large screens mounted high on the wall. However, they should be turned on only when the presenter wants to emphasise a point and then turned off again. Audience members can be distracted or dazzled by the glare of the beam if a presenter is waving their hands around while holding an infra-red pointer that is activated. Infra-red pointers can also greatly magnify nervousness. A small tremor in a presenter's hand can magnify into a spot that jiggles over a metre radius on the screen. Therefore, presenters who think that they will be the least bit nervous should avoid these devices.

Some presentation software packages provide quite sophisticated features. For example, the presenter may be able to draw and write on the screen during the presentation. This can be useful if the presenter wants to add additional information or circle points of interest or to facilitate discussion during the presentation. Presentations can also be conducted over local networks or the Internet. Participants can interact with the presentation by drawing or typing on the screen and the information will be available to all participants. Presentations of this type require careful coordination and a good knowledge of the technology to be effective and therefore should be treated with caution by novice presenters.

6.6.6 Using computer-based presentation software: summary

Excellent presentation software packages are now available to allow presenters to create very professional presentations with ease. To create an effective presentation using these types of software tools it is important to:

- start with the information content and structure, then add the 'sparkle'
- avoid detracting from the central message by using too much 'sparkle'
- ensure that slides have consistent formatting and colour throughout the presentation
- have a thorough understanding of the presentation software from both the creation and presentation points of view
- rehearse the presentation with all of the equipment that will be used

- have a thorough understanding of the presentation technology that will be used in the presentation (projectors, computers, remote controls etc.)
- have a backup plan in case something goes wrong.

6.7 Summary

Earlier chapters focus on written communication techniques. It is essential for contemporary business professionals not only to have good written communication skills but also to develop good oral presentation skills.

Oral presentation is not an easy skill to master, and presenters usually have only one opportunity to deliver their message effectively. Therefore, it is vital that before the presentation the speaker has done sufficient preparation and planning to ensure that the content, visual aids, delivery speed and other key components of the presentation are appropriate for the intended audience. To prepare and deliver effective oral presentations, students should have:

- decided on the purpose of the presentation
- analysed the prospective audience
- decided on the timing of the presentation
- prepared the presentation venue
- structured the presentation appropriately
- prepared effective visual aids
- prepared audience handouts
- practised the presentation.

They should also be confident in:

- handling presentation equipment
- planning for contingencies
- dealing with pre-presentation anxiety
- presenting at an appropriate speed
- gesturing during the presentation
- developing a rapport with the audience
- knowing when and when not to read a speech
- knowing how to stand during the speech
- knowing how humour should be used
- overcoming nervousness
- eliminating annoying habits during the presentation
- presenting in teams
- handling questions from the audience.

These issues have been discussed in detail, and hints and techniques for delivering better presentations have been provided in this chapter.

6.8 Alternatives to oral presentations for distance education students

In some business courses, distance students (including on-line students) will be required to submit 'oral' presentations electronically or in the form of an audiotape or videotape. For these types of presentations, students should apply the same principles and preparation guidelines as outlined here. In these situations, students should attempt to simulate as far as possible a face-to-face presentation, and audiovisual aids may be appropriately integrated into such presentations. It is also important to adhere strictly to any time length guidelines imposed by the instructor. Every attempt should be made to maximise the reproduction quality of such presentations.

7 | Examination techniques[1]

7.1 Introduction

The process of studying for and sitting an examination is a very individual one. Not all techniques work for everyone. The most important thing is to choose the techniques that best suit you, and to decide on a plan of action that will enable you to perform at your best during the examination period. This chapter provides a number of suggestions, hints and techniques that you may adapt to formulate your own plan of attack.

7.2 General hints

7.2.1 When to start studying

Do not leave everything to the last minute. This is a very common and important piece of advice with regard to exams but it is often easier said than done. Learning theory suggests that a steady and routine approach to learning is far better than a period of mad cramming at the end. Furthermore, reliance on short-term memory is illusory: tests have shown that retention rates can be measured in hours, whereas long-term memory becomes more reliable with every reinforcement. Therefore, it makes sense to plan to tackle each of your courses regularly and consistently throughout the semester, and to keep to this plan as far as is practicable.

7.2.2 Revision

The following hints may help you to better plan and prepare for your examinations:

- Revise with a purpose. Find out the exam format; take note of the objectives of the unit, as well as of the individual modules; look at past exam papers for the subject (often available in the library); and review your assignments and the instructor's comments. This information will provide a guide to the likely focus of the exam. Then you will be able to structure your revision around the most important areas, rather than trying to cover everything in the same depth. If, because of extensive revision of subject material, there are no prior exam papers to rely on (or if the whole course is new), then you should ask the instructor for sample questions.

- Find out the exact meaning of terms such as *analyse, comment, compare, contrast, describe, relate, define, distinguish, discuss, explain, illustrate, justify, list, outline, state* and *summarise* (see page 137 for definitions of key instructions).

---

1 This section was originally developed by the late Frank Jarvis; his input is gratefully acknowledged.

- Allow adequate time for revision. If you have not left yourself enough time to cover the material, last-minute cramming may serve only to leave you painfully aware of how much you do not know — and in a state of panic. Once you know your exam timetable, it is a good idea to formulate a study timetable so that you can use your time to greatest advantage.

- Revision should include a variety of activities. Rather than just attempting to commit volumes of information to memory, try to do things a little differently. Attempt past exam questions under exam conditions, or write your own exam questions — you might be surprised by how close you come to the actual exam questions. Produce summaries of summaries so that a word or phrase might trigger your memory; organise regular short study sessions with other students.

- Take regular breaks and allow for adequate rest. It is good to have a balanced approach; try to take some time out for exercise and to eat well. This can break the monotony of study, as well as improving your physical and mental state.

7.3 Pre-examination planning

Make sure you know where and when the exam is to take place. It is essential that you leave yourself plenty of time to get to the exam venue, particularly when some travel is involved. You should also take into account problems of parking, if this applies.

Check that you have all the necessary equipment. Writing materials, erasers, correction fluid, highlighting pens, straight edges, calculators and anything else that is permitted in the exam room should be in good working order (pens run dry, pencils snap, batteries run out).

Check what (if any) written or printed materials are permitted in the exam room, and make sure you have these with you. You should also determine in advance if any qualifications apply (use of highlighter pens, marginal notes or post-it labels may be forbidden).

7.3.1 Perusal time

Use your perusal time wisely. The first thing you must do is read the instructions on the cover page carefully: there have been instances of students failing to notice that they were required to answer only a set number of questions and not the entire paper. Then read the exam script carefully.

If you are given a choice of questions, use this time to decide which ones you will answer and in what order. Work out the time you have to answer each question. (Do this before the exam if you know the format and weightings.) Use the marks allocated to the question as a guide to how much time you will need to answer the question. When working out the timing, leave sufficient time at the end of the exam to review your answers.

If permitted, use perusal time to make brief notes about the questions on the exam paper but not in the exam booklet.

7.3.2 After the examination begins

Try not to panic. Take a deep breath and begin on a question or questions you feel confident about answering. Try doing the questions you feel least confident about second, so that you have them out of the way early on. An alternative approach is to answer short questions first.

Clearly mark the question number or part of the exam that you are answering. Begin each question on a new page. Watch your time carefully. Try not to go over time on any questions, as you may end up with very little time left for the last one or with no time to review your answers. The number of marks allocated will normally be a guide to how long you should spend on the question or part-question. Here are two rules of thumb:

■ allow approximately 30 per cent of the time you have allocated to each question for thinking and organising how you will answer the question

■ periodically check the time you have left but remember that alarm watches are discouraged because they disturb others' concentration.

Do not leave the examination room early: any time you have left over is much better employed reviewing what you have written (see the following). Make sure that you answer each of the questions to the extent expected by the examiner. What is expected in your answer should be clear from the body of the question. Refer to section 7.4 for hints on what the examiner might be expecting for specific types of questions. Make sure you answer the question the examiner has actually asked and make sure you have answered all of the question, not just part of it (refer to the list of key instructions on page 137).

Finally, take a few minutes to check your answers carefully for any silly errors. Return to questions you might have left and attempt them again. Ensure you have entered your name on every exam booklet and have ticked the questions answered in each booklet.

7.4 Content and style of questions

This section gives some useful examples of the styles of question that might be experienced when sitting for an examination. For each style of question, guidelines to the form that appropriate answers should take are offered.

7.4.1 Subject matter limited

Some questions may be worded in a way that limits the subject matter. Answers to these questions should be worded so that they keep strictly to the topic. For example, questions might include the words:

- 'using ... as an example ...'
- 'with respect to ...'
- 'referring to ...'

7.4.2 Scope limited

Some questions may be worded so that the scope is limited. For example:

- 'List four ...'
- 'Evaluate the major impact of ...'
- 'List the main advantages and disadvantages ...'

Answers should once again be restricted to the question's parameters.

7.4.3 Combined subject and scope limited

Some questions may combine scope and subject matter limitation. For example:

- 'Using no more than two examples ...'

Watch for key words in questions that will guide you in how to answer (see p. 137). For example:

- 'What ...' usually indicates that the examiner is testing the scope of your knowledge.
- 'Why ...' or 'How ...' is testing your analytical skills.
- 'Differentiate ...' or 'Compare ...' invites you to present two sides of an argument.

7.4.4 Multiple-choice questions

Be sure to read the question and choices very carefully. If unsure of an answer, use a process of elimination but do not spend too long on a question that you find difficult; return to it at the end.

7.4.5 Short-answer questions

This type of question is designed to elicit brief (one-sentence or, at the most, one-paragraph) responses.

These are distinguished by key instructions such as:

• 'briefly state/discuss, etc . . .'

• 'write short notes on . . .'

• 'explain/expand the following [term/acronym] . . .'

• 'outline . . .'

7.4.6 Point-by-point questions

This type of question is designed to elicit multiline answers, sometimes in a structured form (e.g. 'show in a table'). These are distinguished by key instructions such as:

• 'enumerate . . .'

• 'list . . .'

• 'tabulate . . .'

Be careful to distinguish between key instructions such as *enumerate* and *list*: the former may imply some form of ranking and should elicit a numbered list (1 being the most important); the latter can be answered in bullet points.

Some key instructions, such as *compare* and *contrast*, also lend themselves to answers in tabular form. Be sure to line up your answers logically, as shown:

OBJECT A	OBJECT B
1	1
2	2
3	3

The use of boxes allows you (and the marker) to test the logic of your answer.

7.4.7 Essay-style questions

These questions are designed to elicit multiparagraph, structured answers, depending on the keyword used. Formulate your answers with care. Because of the time constraints, students are often concerned simply with regurgitating as much information as possible in exams. However, even in an exam it is important to follow the usual essay structure of introduction, body and conclusion and to organise your main points in a logical manner. This takes less time than you might think and is actually useful in ensuring that you remember to include important points. It also makes your exam easier to read and better demonstrates your understanding of the subject matter (see chapter 5 for more information about how to approach and write an essay).

Essay-style questions are distinguished by key instructions such as:

- 'discuss ...'
- 'evaluate ...'
- 'debate ...'
- 'analyse ...'
- 'examine critically ...'

7.4.8 Hybrid questions

This type of question is designed to elicit answers that contain an essay component and point-by-point answers. They are distinguished by key instructions such as:

- 'list, giving reasons ...'
- 'draw a model and discuss the major components of the model ...'

7.4.9 Case studies

These are distinguished by a short piece of text followed by questions relating to that text. These questions may be of any type.

Remember to read the text carefully. Use underlining or a highlighter pen to identify key words or phrases (see chapter 4 for more information about how to answer a case study question).

7.4.10 Other types of questions

You may also encounter other forms of questions in examinations. For example, you may be given key instructions such as:

- 'illustrate using diagrams ...'
- 'sketch ...'

These questions are designed to elicit very specific forms of nontext answers. Be sure either to label the components of a diagram or to annotate them and enter the text below the diagram.

7.5 Dos and don'ts when answering examination questions

Dos

- Remember that the people marking your script are only human: try at all times to assist them in evaluating your answers.
- Write legibly (print if your writing is difficult to read). Remember that the marker is not obliged to interpret the answer in your favour.
- Read what you have written. If *you* are unable to make sense of your answer, then the marker will be in the same position.
- Skip to the next question if your mind goes blank. Better still, take a brief rest before skipping.

- Read the question carefully and answer the question that is put to you, not the question you would like to have been put. This is a common failing among students who wish to display their knowledge but do not know the specific answer required.

- Use subheadings in a long answer. As well as showing a logical approach, this makes your answer more readable.

- Leave a blank line after subheadings.

- Leave plenty of space between answers to questions. During the review process you might find that you want to write more and this saves messy bubbles and pointers directing the marker to your afterthoughts.

- Start each question on a new page and number the question correctly.

- Rewrite the answer neatly if too many corrections are needed.

- Use the left page for rough work only. The marker will usually ignore the left page altogether.

Don'ts

- Do not repeat yourself (or the question). Some students write out the question in full. This is a waste of time.

- Do not spend more than your calculated time on any question. If there is time left over you can always return to it.

- Avoid waffle. The point made earlier about spending a significant proportion of your time in planning is reinforced here: a well-planned answer should contain no redundant information.

- Never use words you cannot spell. This is particularly true for words that relate specifically to your discipline area, because it will create a poor impression if you misspell terms you are expected to be familiar with.

- Do not write notes to the marker, particularly rude or facetious ones.

- A new question should not be started at the bottom of a page. The marker might miss an important continuity.

- Never cram a diagram into the last few lines on a page, particularly if you are using an annotated diagram: the marker will have to keep turning the page back and forth.

- Do not write in red on the answer booklet. Because red is the colour generally used by markers, this can cause confusion.

- Never start a new question in the middle of a line. The marker might well miss it or assume that your text refers to the previous question.

7.6 Summary

The examination period can be a very stressful time for students. However, much of the stress associated with exams can be reduced by thorough preparation in the lead-up to the examination. This chapter has provided students with some suggestions on how to study and when to start studying for exams.

Another area where students can increase their chances of success is making effective use of the actual time spent during the examination. A common problem experienced by students is running out of time during examinations with the result that sometimes, entire questions are left unanswered. This usually results in a poor overall performance. A number of useful hints to help students make best use of their time during the examination have been provided in this chapter.

Correct interpretation of exactly what the examiner is asking in a question is another major determinant of success. The way a question is worded will normally give a clear indication of the examiner's expectation in terms of the format and content of the answer. Examples of the various types of questions that a student might encounter, along with examples of possible answers have also been provided to help students to correctly interpret questions.

Another tip when completing an examination script is for the student to make it as easy as possible for the examiner to see that the student knows his or her subject. A list of dos and don'ts that will assist students to ensure that the layout and style of their examination paper is appropriate concludes this chapter.

8 | Winning the 'right' job

8.1 Introduction

Most people are faced with having to apply for a job at least once during their working lives. It was once common for people to remain in one job throughout their entire career but today people tend to change jobs far more frequently.

The competition in today's job market is intense and for some, the process of searching for and ultimately winning a job can be very daunting. However, it can also be very rewarding if approached in the right way. The purpose of this chapter is to help to make the process rewarding for you.

Four main attributes will greatly assist anyone in winning the right job for them.

First, good communications skills are a great asset in any job seeker's toolkit. Good written communication skills are required to document your skills and achievements effectively and good oral communication skills will help you to present yourself and your story in a positive way to a potential employer.

Second, good preparation is vital, both when preparing a curriculum vitae (CV) or resumé and after reaching the interview stage.

Third, presentation plays a large part in whether a job applicant progresses to employee status. Presentation of written documentation is very important. Your CV must be professionally and logically presented and be free of typographical errors. In an interview situation you must also present yourself neatly and professionally.

Fourth, the importance of displaying a positive and enthusiastic attitude at all times cannot be overemphasised. Potential employers will be looking for applicants with a good attitude. In some cases, an applicant with a negative attitude may not be offered a job even if they are strong in other areas.

The stages involved in winning a job can be broadly categorised as:

- The job search
- Preparing 'my story'
- How will I be 'assessed' by my potential employer?
- What do I do after the interview?

These are discussed in the sections that follow.

8.2 The job search

8.2.1 What is the 'right' job?

A job consists of two main parts: what the employee offers and what the employer offers. The employee provides time, knowledge, skills and abilities, effort, commitment and attitude. In exchange, the employer usually offers money, a work environment with appropriate infrastructure, training and career advancement potential. Therefore, the first step in finding the 'right' job is to find a position that has the potential to offer a close match between your personal attributes and expectations and the prospective employer's expectations.

Your own goals and aspirations will influence your ultimate commitment to the job. For example, there is obviously little point in applying for a job that involves a large amount of mathematics if you happen to hate mathematics and have very few skills in that area. Similarly, there may not be much point in applying for a job with no training and no career advancement potential if one of your short-term goals is to increase your skills and advance your career. Therefore, it is very important to make a realistic assessment of the skills and abilities that you have to offer and have a clear understanding of your short- and long-term career goals before starting the search for the 'right' job for you.

8.2.2   How can I find the 'right' job?

Now that you have a better understanding of the type of job that might be 'right' for you, the next step is to find jobs that have the potential to match what you have to offer with the requirements of the particular job.

Places to look for jobs include:

- newspaper advertisements
- 'cold calling'
- placement and recruitment agencies
- the Internet
- your own contacts.

Traditionally, companies have advertised jobs in the 'job vacancies' section of newspapers. Typically, a job advertisement might include a brief outline of the skills required and the role to be undertaken by the successful candidate. An overview of the company might also be included as well as an indication of the potential salary range that a successful applicant might receive. While newspapers are still a valuable source of jobs, many other sources can be explored.

'Cold calling' can be a productive way to indicate your interest in working for an organisation of your choice. This is the process of telephoning, emailing or personally visiting an organisation to apply for a job, even if one is not currently offered. This can be a good way to demonstrate enthusiasm and initiative and can sometimes result in a job offer.

However, many companies now outsource their recruitment to placement or recruitment agencies. The role of these agencies is to find and screen potential candidates for jobs being offered before presenting a short list of applicants to the company offering the job. In many cases, companies will not accept applications that have not been screened by an agency.

The Internet is another good source of jobs. Most recruitment agencies have an on-line presence as well as a physical presence. However, some only accept electronic applications and use automated systems to attempt to match information submitted by the candidate with a list of available jobs on their database. This can help to streamline what can be a very laborious and time-consuming process for both the candidate and the employer but can require a different approach compared with the traditional job placement methods.

Many of the larger organisations have a link on their home page that explains what careers are available with them and how to apply for jobs with the organisation. For example, Gartner, which is an international IT and business consulting organisation, has an extensive amount of information and an on-line résumé submission facility on their *Careers at Gartner* link (www.gartner.com). So if there is a particular organisation that you feel would suit your career needs, look on their home page to see whether it has a *Careers* link.

Personal contacts can also be a rich source of potential jobs. A good place to start might be with friends and family. They will obviously know you well and may be in a position to keep an eye out for potential jobs or even mention your name to employers with whom they are in contact. Business acquaintances and members of sporting or service organisations to which you may belong can also be a good source of employment possibilities. Skills in business networking are well worth developing and there are many good reference materials available on this topic.

Once you have identified one or more jobs that fit your criteria for the 'right' job, you will then need to begin constructing a case to support your belief that you are the best person for the job that is being offered. The stronger your case, the more chance you will have to make the shortlist for an interview, to perform well in subsequent interviews for the job and, ultimately, to be offered the position.

The following section describes how to progress to the interview shortlist by preparing an effective CV.

8.3 Preparing 'my story'

8.3.1 Research the job requirements

The most effective applications and CVs tend to be those that are tailored to suit specific positions, organisations or industries as opposed to résumés that are simply a generic list of previous jobs, education and skills acquired. A major reason specially targeted applications are effective is that they communicate to the people assessing the application that *I know that my skills, education, attitudes and goals fit those specifically required by your organisation and here is some evidence to support that*, rather than *Here is a list of my skills and experience. They may or may not fit those required by your organisation.*

8.3.2 What should my job application contain?

Most job applications will contain at least a covering letter and a CV or résumé. Some may also contain a section that answers key selection criteria or a section containing referees' reports if required.

8.3.3 The covering letter

The covering letter is your way of introducing yourself and letting the person who will be assessing your application know the specific position for which you are applying.

It should be limited to one page and contain your contact details, an accurate description of the position for which you are applying (use the same words as the job information package or advertisement) and a brief discussion on why you think that you are the best person for the position.

Finish with a pleasant concluding paragraph such as 'I look forward to discussing my application further with you.' Use a formal valediction such as *yours sincerely* and make sure that your letter is signed and dated. Note: the generally accepted convention is to use *yours sincerely* when the writer knows the letter recipient, or the letter begins with, for example, *Dear Mr... or Dear Mary*. When the writer does not know the letter recipient, or the letter begins with, for example, *Dear Sir... or Dear Madam,* the more formal *yours faithfully* is appropriate. The valedictions, *regards*, *kind regards* or *best regards* are usually reserved for email correspondence.

The covering letter is your chance to create a good first impression, so make sure that it is professionally presented, has no typographical errors and is clear and concise.

8.3.4 Preparing an effective CV

The first step in preparing an effective CV or résumé is to research the target industry, organisation and position (you will probably have collected at least some information already during your job search phase). The reason for this is so that you have a very clear understanding of what will be required from you as a person working in a particular position for a particular organisation in a particular industry. This information will help you to target your CV effectively.

Sources of information relating to particular industries and organisations include newspapers, the Internet, national stock exchanges (for publicly listed companies) and company annual reports. You can also telephone or email the organisation for specific information. This will give you an idea of what products are produced by the industry or organisation, the size of particular organisations (in terms of staff numbers and turnover) and trends affecting the industry or organisation. Not only will the information that you collect help you to prepare your application but will also mean that you are able to provide informed responses later on when you are offered an interview.

Most organisations will provide an information package describing the specific details of the job on offer. Read this very carefully, and create a list of key points that you will need to deal with in your application. Some organisations (particularly public sector) will provide a list of key selection criteria. When selection criteria are provided, it is a good idea to have a separate document from your CV that specifically answers these criteria. This will be a critical part of your application because organisations that use selection criteria generally base their shortlisting decisions and choice of successful applicant upon how well applicants meet all of the elements outlined in the criteria. An applicant who does not answer the criteria that have been provided will rarely get an interview. (More tips on answering selection criteria are provided in section 8.3.6.)

If selection criteria are not provided, then use the list of key points that you created after reading the information package to present 'your story'.

8.3.5   The format of your CV

The purpose of a CV is to 'paint a picture' of your personal attributes and career history. Specifically, your CV will document your relevant personal details, academic achievements, employment history, career skills and any personal attributes or activities that might be relevant to the position for which you are applying.

A CV can be prepared in one of two basic forms. The first type is referred to as a chronological CV. This is the traditional way that CVs have been presented. The second is called a functional CV. This type of CV can have advantages in terms of being able to target a particular job.

In a chronological CV, information is listed according to when things happened, usually starting with the most recent and finishing with the oldest. One of the advantages of this type of CV is that it provides the reader with a sense of how your career has flowed, when you started and finished the various components of your education and when each of your jobs started and finished. However, on the downside, it can show gaps in your career or inappropriately highlight age or experience.

A functional CV is oriented around particular competencies, skills and experience that you have developed, rather than around when things happened in your career. This type of CV is more difficult to develop than a chronologically arranged CV but works more effectively for applications where you are trying to highlight your suitability for a particular position or target specific roles within an industry. For example, a position may require someone who has good leadership abilities, is a good negotiator and can successfully complete projects on time and to budget. A functionally oriented CV has sections that specifically deal with each of these areas and provide evidence that you have developed strong skills in each of these areas.

Each format has its own strengths and weaknesses and your choice will depend on what aspects of your career that you wish to highlight. Generally, a chronologically arranged CV will be more useful for a person with limited experience but a functionally oriented CV may suit an older person with a wide range of experience.

8.3.6 Answering selection criteria

As mentioned, many employers, particularly public-sector organisations, now specify selection criteria that must be answered satisfactorily before an applicant is shortlisted for an interview.

When an employer provides a list of selection criteria and asks for these to be answered in your application, your goal is to demonstrate that you understand the context of each criterion and that you have the appropriate knowledge, skills or experience to fulfil the requirements of each criterion.

Public sector organisations use very specific terms in drafting selection criteria and it is very important to understand exactly what is meant by the terms before attempting to address the selection criteria. For example, the term *highly developed*, when referring to a particular skill, means that the applicant must have not only used the skills but have used them in a demanding context and done well (Sutcliffe 1998, p. 21).

Each criterion should be answered under a specific heading and must be answered in full. It is important to illustrate how you fulfil each selection criterion, not just make general assertions. It is also important to use active verbs to describe your achievements.

For example, if a selection criterion states that the applicant must have *highly developed project management skills*, a good response might be 'I have ten years' experience in managing projects in the IT sector. The three most complex projects that I have successfully completed include . . . One particularly challenging project that required my specific skills was . . . Although it was a complex and challenging project, I was able to complete the project on time and within budget. Naturally, the clients were very happy with the outcome'.

Non-career-related information can sometimes be used to illustrate your abilities, although make sure that any examples that you use are relevant to the job. For example, in a situation where you are asked to illustrate 'effective leadership abilities' but have no job-related experience to call on, it may be appropriate to include a description of a situation where you have been a member of a services club and have led a team of volunteers in building a playground shelter for a local park. While this is not directly career-related, it does demonstrate that you have had some practical experience in leading a team (and also that you are community minded).

Remember, though, that while it is very important to present your skills and abilities in the best possible light, it is unwise to overstate your abilities or achievements. Your referees' reports and your performance in the interviews to follow will need to support your claims. If they fail to do so, not only will everyone's time be wasted, but your reputation might even be damaged.

8.3.7 Referees' reports

One of the methods of ensuring that applicants do in fact have the attributes and abilities that they claim in their applications and interviews is to ask an independent person or persons who have known the applicant either personally or in a job-related situation to present an assessment of the applicant.

Traditionally, written references were attached to job applications. However, it is now more common simply to include names and contact details on the application and if the applicant successfully makes it to the post-interview shortlist, the referees are contacted either for a written referee's report or for a verbal report, usually by telephone. If you choose to attach a written reference, it is best to include only one unless the employer specifically asks for more. It goes without saying that you should make sure that the reference that you choose is relevant to the job and presents you in the best possible light.

Whether asking for a written report or just using a person's name as a referee, it is very important to ask the potential referee's permission and to allow them sufficient time to prepare. Remember, your referee could play a vital role in attaining the job that you want, so it is very unwise (and bad manners) to get them offside by putting them on the spot. It is also a good idea to provide the referee with some written background about yourself and an overview of the job for which you are applying. In some cases it may even be appropriate to provide them with a copy of your application.

Written reports are usually the best from the applicant's point of view. This provides you with the opportunity to see what has been written about you.

Verbal reports are obviously a little more risky. In most cases you will not be privy to what has been said about you. So if you choose, or are compelled to use, referees who will be interviewed verbally, ensure that they know you well enough and are able to support your case adequately. This is one of the reasons it is sensible to provide referees with adequate background information before they are asked by your prospective employer to comment on you.

8.3.8 Dos and don'ts

Dos

- Make sure that you thoroughly research the industry, organisation and position.
- Present your job application professionally.
- Be concise.
- Remove all grammatical and typographical errors.
- Ask potential referees' permission in plenty of time before your application is submitted.
- Tailor your application to the specific job.
- Ensure that if you are required to answer selection criteria that you answer each criterion in its entirety.
- Use action verbs to illustrate your skills and abilities.

- Make sure that you fully understand the job requirements before putting together your application.

- Proofread (and, preferably, have someone else proofread) your application before submitting.

Don'ts

- Do not ramble on.

- Do not include irrelevant information.

- Do not overstate your skills and abilities.

8.3.9 Summary

Remember that your job application will create an image of you in the reader's mind. Your objective is to make it a positive one. By properly researching the background of the position for which you are applying and creating a professionally presented, targeted job application, you will present yourself in the best possible way to the reader. You should then have a good chance to move on to the next stage in the process.

In some cases, for example, if you are applying for a position through a recruitment agency, the next step may be to undergo psychometric testing (this is described in section 8.4.7). However, you may progress directly to the interview stage. The next section describes how your prospective employer may assess you for suitability for the position being offered.

8.4 How will I be 'assessed' by my potential employer?

8.4.1 Preparation

Not surprisingly, preparation is a vital component at this stage as well. It is arguably even more important at this stage than in earlier stages.

During preparation of the job application you have plenty of time to think about what you would like to include in it. You even have the opportunity to go over it as many times as is necessary to produce a polished, final product. In an interview situation, you will not be afforded that luxury. In most cases, you will only have one opportunity to respond. Therefore, you will need to think 'on your feet' and formulate appropriate responses to questions quickly and confidently. This means that you must be well prepared. Long pauses, contradictions, superficial responses, irrelevancies and repetition tend not to leave a favourable impression in the interviewer's mind. These can all result from inadequate preparation.

It is obvious that you will be expected to have a thorough knowledge of your own career history, so make sure that you know exactly what is in your job application. Remember to make sure that what you say in a job interview does not contradict what you have stated in your job application. As mentioned, it is important not to overstate your abilities or achievements in your job application because the interviewer will be looking to confirm in the interview what you have claimed in your application. Glaring inconsistencies in what you have said you can do and how you perform in an interview will definitely not present you in the best possible light.

It is also important to have at least some knowledge of the organisation and the industry in which you wish to work. This will allow you to provide informed responses to industry-related questions.

You will have already done much of the preparation for this stage in preparing your job application but make sure that you spend time reviewing your research before going to the interview.

Another important part of preparing for the interview is to confirm exactly when and where the interview will take place. It is also important to know how many people are likely to be conducting the interview and, if possible, find out their names and roles within the organisation. This information can usually be obtained from the human resources department of the organisation where the job is being offered.

8.4.2 The interview

You will be required to participate in at least one and possibly two or more interviews before being selected for a position.

The first interview may take the form of an 'informal chat', either in person or on the telephone. Even though this type of interview is regarded as being informal, you are already being assessed as a potential candidate and, therefore, it is important to conduct yourself as you would in a 'formal' interview.

The second and subsequent interviews will normally be conducted formally with either a single interviewer, or more commonly, a panel of interviewers. A panel will normally consist of a representative from the human resources department and one or more people, either for, or with whom you may be working should you be successful in obtaining the position.

It is very important to be punctual, to dress appropriately and to present yourself professionally when attending an interview. First impressions remain, so make sure that they are positive.

Being late for an interview may suggest that you will always be late and presents a very poor first impression. Make sure that you know exactly when and where the interview will be conducted and leave yourself adequate time to get to the interview at least ten minutes early. There is nothing worse than being flustered because you have been delayed in traffic or because you have not been able to find the building where the interview is to be conducted.

Dressing too casually can cause the interviewers to form the view that you are sloppy and unprofessional. Generally, a good rule of thumb is to dress according to the culture of the organisation but, if in doubt, err on the formal side. Neat, formal dress always looks professional. Loud clothing or ultrastrong perfumes can give the wrong impression.

Remember that your goal in the interview is to display enthusiasm, competence and a positive attitude. However, it is important not to go 'over the top'. Boisterous behaviour, loud laughter, discussion of controversial issues and rude jokes are not usually considered to be appropriate in an interview situation, so this sort of behaviour should definitely be avoided.

Negative discussion of other people and organisations, particularly previous employers should also be avoided. This does not convey a positive attitude.

Make sure that you turn off your mobile phone before entering the interview room. A ringing phone does not give the impression that you are an important person. On the contrary, it will simply disrupt the whole interview and is a sign of bad manners.

When entering the interview room, greet the interviewers warmly and shake hands with each of them, then wait to be asked before being seated. Your handshake should be firm without crushing the other person's fingers.

During the interview, maintain eye contact with the person asking the question but remember to include the other members of the panel too. Refer to the interviewers formally (i.e. with a title and surname), unless specifically asked by them to use first names.

When asked a question, take a moment to collect your thoughts then respond clearly and confidently. Try not to ramble or repeat yourself. Generally, the interviewers will have a busy schedule and time wasters will be viewed negatively.

8.4.3   Questions that can be difficult to handle

One of the types of questions that is often handled very badly but can be a very good opportunity to paint a positive image in the mind of the interviewer is the open-ended question.

An example of an open-ended question is *Can you describe yourself for me?* A similar question will usually turn up in every interview, so make sure that you have a well-prepared response. The idea is to tell a small story that highlights your main strengths and attributes and subtly links these to the requirements of the job for which you are applying.

Your story might start with a brief overview of relevant academic achievements, then move to two or three career-related projects or problem scenarios that highlight your strengths. First, give a brief background to the problem or project, then describe how you went about solving the problem or carrying out the project, finally describe the outcome (make sure that you choose a problem or project where there was a positive outcome). Keep your story brief but be expansive enough to provide a complete and positive picture of your abilities for the interview panel.

Another difficult question to handle is one such as *Describe a situation in your career where you think things went badly* or *What are your worst characteristics?* In this type of question you are being asked to describe either your weaknesses or your career-related failures and a poor answer can destroy any chance of further progress for you. It is not a good idea in this situation to take the opportunity to list every one of your character flaws or discuss every last incident that went badly during your career. However, it is worth remembering that no-one is perfect and providing an answer that suggests that nothing has ever gone wrong in your career and that you have no weaknesses, probably will be regarded by the interview panel with some skepticism. A better approach is to select a genuine incident, preferably early in your career, that did not go as well as you would have liked, briefly describe how you handled the situation, what you learnt from the experience and how it has strengthened your ability to handle similar situations. You could also describe an area where you are not as strong and describe measures that you have taken to address the issue. For example, 'I have always found it difficult to present to large audiences. However, six months ago I joined a Toastmasters club and my last two presentations have been very well received'. This shows that you have recognised a weakness and have taken steps to improve your skills.

Again, good preparation is vital in providing confident answers to interview questions.

8.4.4   Telephone interviews

In some cases, for example, when the interview candidates are overseas or where it is not practical for candidates to be interviewed face-to-face, interviews are conducted by telephone.

This type of interview can be more difficult than a face-to-face interview, primarily because the interviewee cannot actually see the interviewers and vice versa. Therefore, some of the normal feedback mechanisms, such as body language, are eliminated. In a face-to-face interview it is possible to 'read' how the interview is proceeding by watching the reactions of the interviewers. This is much more difficult over the telephone.

Bad communications lines can also affect the flow of the interview and can in some cases cause inappropriate responses to be given if the question has not been fully understood. Therefore, it is important when being interviewed over the telephone to speak clearly when responding and to clarify any questions that are unclear.

Because the interviewers cannot see your face, it is important to make sure that your voice has a pleasant and expressive tone. A monotonous tone on the telephone can cause an interviewer's concentration to wander and they may miss some important information. You must also stay alert to ensure that you do not miss any information.

If you are unsure whether you have conveyed your message adequately, you should also get some feedback from the interviewer. For example, if you ask *Have I covered the points that you were looking for?*, the interviewer then has the opportunity to say something similar to *No, that's not exactly what I was getting at. Can you tell me more about . . .?* if there is something else that they would like clarified. Otherwise, an important opportunity to expand on your strengths might be lost.

8.4.5 Bring the interview to a conclusion

When the interview is about to be concluded, the interviewer will usually ask whether there is anything further that you would like to say or whether there are any questions that you would like to ask.

This is not the signal to ask 50 questions about the position or to discuss, in intricate detail, how much you will be paid and how often you can expect a payrise. Most of these questions can be clarified after you have been offered the position.

It is, however, a good opportunity to succinctly summarise why you think you are suitable for the position and why you would like the position. Take care not to take up too much time. Tapping of pens and shuffling of papers is a good indication that the interviewers are keen to move on to the next interview. Heed those warnings.

Before leaving the room, shake hands with each of the interviewers and thank them for their time.

8.4.6 Dos and don'ts

Dos

- Prepare thoroughly.
- Be on time for the interview.

- Dress and act professionally at all times.

- Prepare responses to open-ended questions.

- Be courteous to the interviewers.

- Display a positive attitude.

- Turn off your mobile phone before entering the interview.

- Conclude the interview gracefully.

Don'ts

- Do not dress too casually.

- Do not make negative comments about former employers, organisations or workmates.

- Do not take up the interviewers' time with irrelevancies.

- Do not try to give 'off the cuff' responses to open-ended questions.

- Do not overstay your welcome.

8.4.7　Psychometric testing

Psychometric or psychological testing is used widely today to assess the suitability of candidates in the recruitment process. Sometimes, this type of testing will be conducted before the candidate is offered an interview, and sometimes the tests will be conducted before proceeding to the final interview stage.

These types of tests are designed to assess a candidate on a number of levels. Some tests attempt to assess the candidate's personality type in terms of whether they are, for example, leaders or whether they like to work alone or in teams. Other tests assess a candidate's general intelligence (e.g. IQ testing). Candidates can also be assessed in terms of their abilities to carry out job-related activities (e.g. mathematical abilities, typing speed).

Psychometric tests generally take the form of a question with several potential responses. For example, the Myers Briggs questionnaire includes 126 questions and attempts to categorise the respondent's responses according to 16 possible personality type combinations (extrovert/introvert, sensing/intuitive, thinking/feeling, judging/perceiving), which have specific definitions. For example, someone might be categorised as ESTJ: (e)xtrovert, (s)ensing, (t)hinking, (j)udging (Jones 1993, pp. 52–8).

Another type of test, the PA preference inventory or PAPI test, presents 90 pairs of statements to the respondent (e.g. *I am a hard worker* or *I am not moody*). The respondent must choose the statement that most closely describes them at work. The test has been devised to reveal the nature of a person's preferred way of working and how they might fit in a particular organisation (Jones 1993, pp. 45–51).

These are just two examples of a large range of tests that organisations can use in the recruitment process. The main things to remember about these types of tests are that there are generally no right or wrong answers and that they are not designed to interrogate people or provide a deep psychoanalysis. The main reason for their use is to determine reasonably efficiently how a potential candidate might fit into an organisation or role, or to choose one or more suitable candidates from a large number of applicants.

It is also important to note that it is difficult to 'fake' responses to psychometric tests. A number of questions are usually inserted to identify attempts to fake a particular personality type or personal attribute.

Many reference books and websites provide information about specific tests. Some even provide practice questions.

8.5 Social networking sites

Internet-based social networking sites and on-line communities such as Facebook, MySpace and LinkedIn are being used more and more as resources in employers' recruitment toolkits. These sites can be used by employers to either place job advertisements, search for suitable candidates, or screen potential candidates. Sites such as these can provide fantastic opportunities to connect with family and friends. However, there is also a hidden downside to putting your personal information in the public domain. As part of the screening process, a potential employer who accesses information that you have posted may be able to build a profile about you that could hinder your job prospects. It is therefore well worth considering in this context, each story, video or photo that you post to social networking sites.

8.6 What do I do after the interview?

Following up with a thank-you note or email one or two days after your interview is not only good manners but also shows the interviewer that you appreciate his or her time. It also serves to reinforce your name in the interviewer's mind and demonstrates that you are keen to take up the challenge of the job. But keep the communication brief. It is not meant to be a rehash of your entire job application.

Eventually, you will either be offered the job or will receive notice that you have been unsuccessful. If you have been successful, you will obviously be faced with the happy decision as to whether or not to accept the position.

If you are unsuccessful, try not to take the news negatively. Use the experience to help you to perform better at your next opportunity. Go over your interview while it is still fresh in your mind to attempt to identify where you could improve and attach notes to your file copy of the job application for later reference.

It is also worth, if possible, telephoning the interviewer or panel chairperson to find out why you were unsuccessful. If you are able to contact someone from the interview panel, it is not appropriate to argue your case or become involved in a heated discussion. Your objective is to find out in a positive and constructive manner, if there are any areas that would strengthen your chances of being successful in the future. Most people will be helpful and constructive if approached in the right manner.

8.7 Summary

The process of applying for a job and navigating through the interview and assessment process can be stressful or rewarding (sometimes both).

Obviously, a prerequisite for being successful in any job application is having the requisite skills, personal attributes and academic achievements. However, this chapter has emphasised four key attributes that will help to take an application beyond the basics: good communication skills, solid preparation, professional presentation and a positive and enthusiastic attitude. The chapter has also outlined each of the steps in the job search, starting from the research phase through to preparing an effective application and finally successfully navigating the interview process.

By making an effort to ensure that you have addressed the four key attributes and by applying the hints included in the chapter, you will greatly strengthen your chances of winning the 'right' job.

8.8 List of references

Byron, M 1994, *How to pass graduate recruitment tests*, Kogan Page, London.

Dale, M 1995, *Successful recruitment and selection A practical guide for managers*, Kogan Page, London.

Jones, S 1993, *Psychological testing for managers: a complete guide to using and surviving 19 popular recruitment and career development tests*, Judy Piatkus Publishers, London.

Leanne, S 2004, *How to interview like a top MBA: job-winning strategies from headhunters, Fortune 100 recruiters and career counselors*, McGraw-Hill, New York.

Sutcliffe, K 1998, *Open the door to your future: getting interviews and jobs in Australia*, Brolga Press, Gundaroo, NSW.

Resources

Key instructions

Analyse	Show the essence of something by breaking it down into component parts, examining each part in detail and showing how the parts fit together.
Argue	Present the case for and/or against a particular proposition.
Compare	Look for similarities between propositions or objects.
Contrast	Look for differences between propositions or objects.
Criticise	Give your judgement, backed by a discussion of the evidence, on the merit of theories or opinions or the truth of 'facts'.
Debate	Argue from two or more viewpoints.
Define	Set down the precise meaning of a word or phrase. Show that the distinctions implied in the definition are necessary.
Describe	Give a detailed or graphic account of.
Differentiate	As for 'distinguish'.
Discuss	Investigate or examine by argument; sift and debate, giving reasons for and against.
Distinguish	Find differences between two or more apparently different propositions, ideas or objects.
Draw	1. Make a diagram of (an object). 2. Argue for or against a proposition, producing 'a/some conclusion(s) from it'.
Enumerate	List or specify and describe in a structured manner, and prioritise.
Evaluate	Make an appraisal of the worth of something, in the light of its apparent truth or utility; include your personal opinion.
Examine	Present in depth and investigate the implications of.
Expand	Give the full meaning of an acronym or abbreviation.
Explain	Make plain; interpret and account for in detail.
Illustrate	Explain and make clear using concrete written examples or a figure or diagram.
Interpret	Bring out the meaning of, and make clear and explicit, usually also giving your own judgement.
Justify	Show adequate grounds for decisions or conclusions.
Outline	Give the main features or general principles of a subject, omitting minor details, and emphasising structure and relationship.
Prove	1. Demonstrate the truth or falsity by presenting evidence. 2. Provide a mathematical/logical proof.
Relate	Narrate/show how things are connected to each other and to what extent they are alike or affect each other.
Review	Make a survey of, examining the subject critically.
Sketch	Draw a freehand picture.

State	Specify fully and clearly.
Summarise	Give a concise account of the chief points or substance of a matter, omitting details and examples.
Trace	Identify and describe the development or history of a topic from some point or origin.

(Adapted from Queensland University of Technology 1988, *The written assignment*, Brisbane, p. 27)

List of references

Deakin University 1993, *Faculty of Arts style guide*, Geelong.

Elms, J 1993, *Essay assignments: a user friendly guide*, University of Southern Queensland Student Association, Toowoomba.

Lovell, DW & Moore, RD 1993, *Essay writing and style guide for politics and the social sciences,* Australian Political Studies Association, Canberra.

Mandel, S 1993, *Effective presentation skills: a practical guide for better speaking*, Career Builders, Brisbane.

Perry, C (n.d.), *A structured approach to presenting PhD theses: notes for candidates and their supervisors*, unpublished paper, School of Marketing, Advertising and Public Relations, Queensland University of Technology.

Queensland University of Technology 1989, *The written assignment*, Brisbane.

Style manual for authors, editors and printers 2002, 6th edn, John Wiley & Sons, Brisbane.

University of Queensland, Gatton College 1994, *A guide to preparing and presenting written assignments*, eds J. Summers and C. Pedersen, Department of Business Studies, Gatton.

University of Southern Queensland 1994, *Communications*, Distance Education Centre, Toowoomba.

Index